P9-AQR-735

21ST CENTURY HEALTH
AND WELLNESS

The
Human Body:
An Overview

Mary Kittredge

Introduction by C. Everett Koop, M.D., Sc.D.
Former Surgeon General, U.S. Public Health Service
Foreword by Sandra Thurman
Director, Office of National AIDS Policy, The White House

CHELSEA HOUSE PUBLISHERS
Philadelphia

The goal of *21ST CENTURY HEALTH AND WELLNESS* is to provide general information in the ever-changing areas of physiology, psychology, and related medical issues. The titles in this series are not intended to take the place of the professional advice of a physician or other health-care professional.

Chelsea House Publishers
EDITOR IN CHIEF: Stephen Reginald
PRODUCTION MANAGER: Pamela Loos
ART DIRECTOR: Sara Davis
DIRECTOR OF PHOTOGRAPHY: Judy Hasday
MANAGING EDITOR: James D. Gallagher
SENIOR PRODUCTION EDITOR: J. Christopher Higgins
ASSISTANT EDITOR: Anne Hill
PRODUCTION SERVICES: Pre-Press Company, Inc.
COVER DESIGNER/ILLUSTRATOR: Emiliano Begnardi

The Chelsea House World Wide Web site address is http://www.chelseahouse.com

1 3 5 7 9 8 6 4 2

Library of Congress Cataloging-in-Publication Data

Kittredge, Mary, 1949–
The human body : an overview / Mary Kittredge ; introduction by C. Everett Koop ;
foreword by Sandra Thurman.
p. cm. — (21st century health and wellness)
Includes bibliographical references and index.
ISBN 0-7910-5980-4
1. Human physiology. 2. Body, Human. I. Title. II Series.

QP34.5 .K57 2000
612—dc21

00-024079

CONTENTS

21ST CENTURY HEALTH AND WELLNESS

PREVENTION AND EDUCATION: THE KEYS TO GOOD HEALTH

C. Everett Koop, M.D., Sc.D.
FORMER SURGEON GENERAL,
U.S. Public Health Service

The issue of health education has received particular attention in recent years because of the presence of AIDS in the news. But our response to this particular tragedy points up a number of broader issues that doctors, public health officials, educators, and the public face. In particular, it spotlights the importance of sound health education for citizens of all ages.

Over the past 35 years, this country has been able to achieve dramatic declines in the death rates from heart disease, stroke, accidents, and—for people under the age of 45—cancer. Today, Americans generally eat better and take better care of themselves than ever before. Thus, with the help of modern science and technology, they have a better chance of surviving serious—even catastrophic—illnesses. In 1996, the life expectancy of Americans reached an all-time high of 76.1 years. That's the good news.

The flip side of this advance has special significance for young adults. According to a report issued in 1998 by the U.S. Department of Health and Human Services, levels of wealth and education in the United States are directly correlated with our population's health. The more money Americans make and the more years of schooling they have, the better their health will be. Furthermore, income inequality increased in the U.S. between 1970 and 1996. Basically, the rich got richer—people in high income brackets had greater increases in the amount of money made than did those at low income levels. In addition, the report indicated that children under 18 are more likely to live in poverty than the population as a whole.

Family income rises with each higher level of education for both men and women from every ethnic and racial background. Life expectancy, too, is related to family income. People with lower incomes tend to die at younger ages than people from more affluent homes. What all this means is that health is a factor of wealth and education, both of which need to be improved for all Americans if the promise of life, liberty, and the pursuit of happiness is to include an equal chance for good health.

The health of young people is further threatened by violent death and injury, alcohol and drug abuse, unwanted pregnancies, and sexually transmitted diseases. Adolescents are particularly vulnerable because they are beginning to explore their own sexuality and perhaps to experiment with drugs and alcohol. We need to educate young people to avoid serious dangers to their health. The price of neglect is high.

Even for the population as a whole, health is still far from what it could be. Why? Most death and disease are attributed to four broad elements: inadequacies in the health-care system, behavioral factors or unhealthy lifestyles, environmental hazards, and human biological factors. These categories are also influenced by individual resources. For example, low birth weight and infant mortality are more common among the children of less educated mothers. Likewise, women with more education are more likely to obtain prenatal care during pregnancy. Mothers with fewer than 12 years of education are almost 10 times more likely to smoke during pregnancy—and new studies find excessive aggression later in life as well as other physical ailments among the children of smokers. In short, poor people with less education are more likely to smoke cigarettes, which endangers health and shortens the life span. About a third of the children who begin smoking will eventually have their lives cut short because of this practice.

Similarly, poor children are exposed more often to environmental lead, which causes a wide range of physical and mental problems. Sedentary lifestyles are also more common among teens with lower family income than among wealthier adolescents. Being overweight—a condition associated with physical inactivity as well as excessive caloric intake—is also more common among poor, non-Hispanic, white adolescents. Children from rich families are more likely to have health insurance. Therefore, they are more apt to receive vaccinations and other forms of early preventative medicine and treatment. The bottom line is that kids from lower income groups receive less adequate health care.

To be sure, some diseases are still beyond the control of even the most advanced medical techniques that our richest citizens can afford. Despite yearnings that are as old as the human race itself, there is no "fountain of youth" to prevent aging and death. Still, solutions are available for many of the problems that undermine sound health. In a word, that solution is prevention. Prevention, which includes health promotion and education, can save lives, improve the quality of life, and, in the long run, save money.

In the United States, organized public health activities and preventative medicine have a long history. Important milestones include the improvement of sanitary procedures and the development of pasteurized milk in the late-19th century, and the introduction in the mid-20th century of effective vaccines against polio, measles, German measles, mumps, and other once-rampant diseases. Internationally, organized public health efforts began on a wide-scale basis with the International Sanitary Conference of 1851, to which 12 nations sent representatives. The World Health Organization, founded in 1948, continues these efforts under the aegis of the United Nations, with particular emphasis on combating communicable diseases and the training of health-care workers.

Despite these accomplishments, much remains to be done in the field of prevention. For too long, we have had a medical system that is science and technology-based, and focuses essentially on illness and mortality. It is now patently obvious that both the social and the economic costs of such a system are becoming insupportable.

Implementing prevention and its corollaries, health education and health promotion, is the job of several groups of people. First, the medical and scientific professions need to continue basic scientific research, and here we are making considerable progress. But increased concern with prevention will also have a decided impact on how primary-care doctors practice medicine. With a shift to health-based rather than morbidity-based medicine, the role of the "new physician" includes a healthy dose of patient education.

Second, practitioners of the social and behavioral sciences—psychologists, economists, and city planners along with lawyers, business leaders, and government officials—must solve the practical and ethical dilemmas confronting us: poverty, crime, civil rights, literacy, education, employment, housing, sanitation, environmental protection, health-care delivery systems, and so forth. All of these issues affect public health.

Third is the public at large. We consider this group to be important in any movement. Fourth, and the linchpin in this effort, is the public health profession: doctors, epidemiologists, teachers—who must harness the professional expertise of the first two groups and the common sense and cooperation of the third: the public. They must define the problems statistically and qualitatively and then help set priorities for finding solutions.

To a very large extent, improving health statistics is the responsibility of every individual. So let's consider more specifically what the role of the individual should be and why health education is so important. First, and most obviously, individuals can protect themselves from illness and injury and thus minimize the need for professional medical care. They can eat a nutritious diet; get adequate exercise; avoid tobacco, alcohol, and drugs; and take prudent steps to avoid accidents. The proverbial "apple a day keeps the doctor away" is not so far from the truth, after all.

Second, individuals should actively participate in their own medical care. They should schedule regular medical and dental checkups. If an illness or injury develops, they should know when to treat themselves and when to seek professional help. To gain the maximum benefit from any medical treatment, individuals must become partners in treatment. For instance, they should understand the effects and side effects of medications. I counsel young physicians that there is no such thing as too much information when talking with patients. But the corollary is the patient must know enough about the nuts and bolts of the healing process to understand what the doctor is telling him or her. That responsibility is at least partially the patient's.

Education is equally necessary for us to understand the ethical and public policy issues in health care today. Sometimes individuals will encounter these issues in making decisions about their own treatment or that of family members. Other citizens may encounter them as jurors in medical malpractice cases. But we all become involved, indirectly, when we elect our public officials, from school board members to the president. Should surrogate parenting be legal? To what extent is drug testing desirable, legal, or necessary? Should there be public funding for family planning, hospitals, various types of medical research, and medical care for the indigent? How should we allocate scant technological resources, such as kidney dialysis and organ transplants? What is the proper role of government in protecting the rights of patients?

What are the broad goals of public health in the United States today? The Public Health Service has defined these goals in terms of mortality, education, and health improvement. It identified 15 major concerns: controlling high blood pressure, improving family planning, pregnancy care and infant health, increasing the rate of immunization, controlling sexually transmitted diseases, controlling the presence of toxic agents or radiation in the environment, improving occupational safety and health, preventing accidents, promoting water fluoridation and dental health, controlling infectious diseases, decreasing smoking, decreasing alcohol and drug abuse, improving nutrition, promoting physical fitness and exercise, and controlling stress and violent behavior. Great progress has been made in many of these areas. For example, the report *Health, United States, 1998* indicates that in general, the workplace is safer today than it was a decade ago. Between 1980 and 1993, the overall death rate from occupational injuries dropped 45 percent to 4.2 deaths per 100,000 workers.

For healthy adolescents and young adults (ages 15 to 24), the specific goal defined by the Public Health Service was a 20% reduction in deaths, with a special focus on motor vehicle injuries as well as alcohol and drug abuse. For adults (ages 25 to 64), the aim was 25% fewer deaths, with a concentration on heart attacks, strokes, and cancers. In the 1999 National Drug Control Strategy, the White House Office of National Drug Control Policy echoed the Congressional goal of reducing drug use by 50 percent in the coming decade.

Smoking is perhaps the best example of how individual behavior can have a direct impact on health. Today cigarette smoking is recognized as the most important single preventable cause of death in our society. It is responsible for more cancers and more cancer deaths than any other known agent; is a prime risk factor for heart and blood vessel disease, chronic bronchitis, and emphysema; and is a frequent cause of complications in pregnancies and of babies born prematurely, underweight, or with potentially fatal respiratory and cardiovascular problems.

Since the release of the Surgeon General's first report on smoking in 1964, the proportion of adult smokers has declined substantially, from 43% in 1965 to 30.5% in 1985. The rate of cigarette smoking among adults declined from 1974 to 1995, but rates of decline were greater among the more educated. Since 1965, more than 50 million people have quit smoking. Although the rate of adult smoking has decreased, children and teenagers are smoking more. Researchers have also noted a disturbing correlation between underage smoking of cigarettes and later use of cocaine and heroin. Although there is still much work to be done if we are to become a "smoke free society," it is heartening to note that public health and public education efforts—such as warnings on cigarette packages, bans on broadcast advertising, removal of billboards advertising cigarettes, and anti-drug youth campaigns in the media— have already had significant effects.

In 1997, the first leveling off of drug use since 1992 was found in eighth graders, with marijuana use in the past month declining to 10 percent. The percentage of eighth graders who drink alcohol or smoke cigarettes also decreased slightly in 1997. In 1994 and 1995, there were more than 142,000 cocaine-related emergency-room episodes per year, the highest number ever reported since these events were tracked starting in 1978. Illegal drugs present a serious threat to Americans who use these drugs. Addiction is a chronic, relapsing disease that changes the chemistry of the brain in harmful ways. The abuse of inhalants and solvents found in legal products like hair spray, paint thinner, and industrial cleaners—called "huffing" (through the mouth) or "sniffing" (through the nose)—has come to public attention in recent years. *The National Household Survey on Drug Abuse* discovered that among youngsters ages 12 to 17, this dangerous practice doubled between 1991 and 1996 from 10.3 percent to 21 percent. An alarming large number of children died the very first time they tried inhalants, which can also cause brain damage or injure other vital organs.

Another threat to public health comes from firearm injuries. Fortunately, the number of such assaults declined between 1993 and 1996. Nevertheless, excessive violence in our culture—as depicted in the mass media—may have contributed to the random shootings at Columbine High School in Littleton, Colorado, and elsewhere. The government and private citizens are rethinking how to reduce the fascination with violence so that America can become a safer, healthier place to live.

The "smart money" is on improving health care for everyone. Only recently did we realize that the gap between the "haves" and "have-nots" had a significant health component. One more reason to invest in education is that schooling produces better health.

In 1835, Alexis de Tocqueville, a French visitor to America, wrote, "In America, the passion for physical well-being is general." Today, as then, health and fitness are front-page items. But with the greater scientific and technological resources now available to us, we are in a far stronger position to make good health care available to everyone. With the greater technological threats to us as we approach the 21st century, the need to do so is more urgent than ever before. Comprehensive information about basic biology, preventative medicine, medical and surgical treatments, and related ethical and public policy issues can help you arm yourself with adequate knowledge to be healthy throughout life.

FOREWORD

Sandra Thurman, Director, Office of National AIDS Policy, The White House

A hundred years ago, an era was marked by discovery, invention, and the infinite possibilities of progress. Nothing piqued society's curiosity more than the mysterious workings of the human body. They poked and prodded, experimented with new remedies and discarded old ones, increased longevity and reduced death rates. But not even the most enterprising minds of the day could have dreamed of the advancements that would soon become our shared reality. Could they have envisioned that we would vaccinate millions of children against polio? Ward off the annoyance of allergy season with a single pill? Or give life to a heart that had stopped keeping time?

As we stand on the brink of a new millennium, the progress made during the last hundred years is indeed staggering. And we continue to push forward every minute of every day. We now exist in a working global community, blasting through cyber-space at the speed of light, sharing knowledge and up-to-the-minute technology. We are in a unique position to benefit from the world's rich fabric of traditional healing practices while continuing to explore advances in modern medicine. In the halls of our medical schools, tomorrow's healers are learning to appreciate the complexities of our whole person. We are not only keeping people alive, we are keeping them well.

Although we deserve to rejoice in our progress, we must also remember that our health remains a complex web. Our world changes with each step forward and we are continuously faced with new threats to our well-being. The air we breathe has become polluted, the water tainted, and new killers have emerged to challenge us in ways we are just beginning to understand. AIDS, in particular, continues to tighten its grip on America's most fragile communities, and place our next generation in jeopardy.

Facing these new challenges will require us to find inventive ways to stay healthy. We already know the dangers of alcohol, smoking and drug abuse. We also understand the benefits of early detection for illnesses like cancer and heart disease, two areas where scientists have made significant in-roads to treatment. We have become a well-informed society, and with that information comes a renewed emphasis on preventative care and a sense of personal responsibility to care for both ourselves and those who need our help.

Read. Re-read. Study. Explore the amazing working machine that is the human body. Share with your friends and your families what you have learned. It is up to all of us living together as a community to care for our well-being, and to continue working for a healthier quality of life.

THE PERFECT MACHINE

In the 20th century, human beings built the most complex and powerful machines ever known: computers that solve problems of great difficulty, rocket ships able to fly to the moon and beyond, and manufacturing equipment to produce useful things efficiently and cheaply—to mention only a few. Yet no machine made by human beings has equaled the complexity and power of the human body itself.

Each human body begins as a single cell, and just nine months later it will have grown to billions of cells. By the time a new human being is born, the cells have become specialized and grouped together to form the tissues, organs, and systems that give the body its many remarkable abilities.

Some parts of the body detect light, others detect sound vibrations. Still others sense heat, cold, pressure, and other information about the world. A complicated communication center, the brain, makes sense of this information while handling messages to and from the body via an enormous information network. Along the network's 10 billion message-transmitting cells, tiny electrical impulses move at speeds of up to 200 miles per hour.

Other body parts take in food, oxygen, and water and circulate these substances to the sites where they are processed into fuel and used. The main pump for the body's circulation, the heart, is so reliable that it can beat at the rate of 70 times per minute throughout a person's whole life—a total of 2½ billion heartbeats to pump a lifetime's supply of blood: 55 million gallons. The wastes from the body's fuel-burning operation are efficiently disposed of, too, maintaining a balance between food coming in and waste products going out.

Still other structures allow the body to move about: to walk or jog, sit or stand, fight or run away. The body's strength and mobility is so great, in fact, that the average adult walks about eight miles each day without even noticing the effort. The body defends itself against diseases and repairs at least some of its own injuries, as well. And the body is capable of reproduction, creating from itself the new cell that, once released or fertilized, will grow and change into yet another whole human being. Finally, the body fine-tunes many of its own operations through the use of chemicals that it produces for itself.

If the human body were a machine, one would surely think that it was wonderful. But the body is more remarkable still, for in addition to all its other complex parts and functions, the human body has awareness. Its systems make up a whole person, one who can think, remember, form plans, and feel emotions like wonder, sorrow, and love. Unlike a machine, a human being is aware of the world and of him- or herself.

The human body is different from a machine in that it has the ability to feel emotions such as love.

This book is meant to help young people and those who care for them learn more about the human body. In it they will discover what our ancestors thought about the body and how scientists throughout the ages have uncovered many of its secrets. They will learn about the cell, the building block of all living things; about human tissues, collections of cells that organize for specific purposes in the body; and about the body's organs and organ systems, specialized parts that cooperate to make the body as a whole work. They will also learn how the human body reproduces, creating a new person from the joining together of two parents. Finally, they will learn how scientists continue to explore the human body, revealing even more of its remarkable mysteries, and how current research may help make the bodies of future human beings even stronger and healthier than the ones people have today.

1

THE HUMAN BODY IN HISTORY

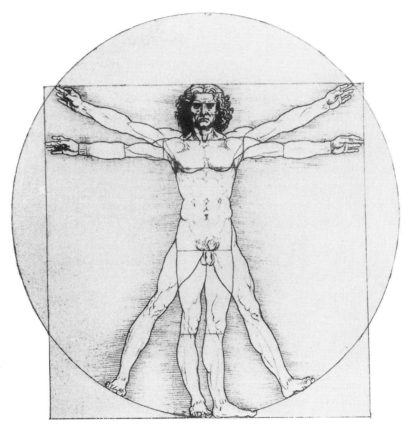

An anatomical drawing of the male figure by Leonardo da Vinci.

Mﾠore than 12,000 years ago, primitive healers of the Paleolithic era (the Stone Age, 2.5 million to 10,000 years ago) performed crude brain surgery, cutting holes in patients' skulls in a process now called *trephination*. This Stone Age surgery was not based on a scientific idea of the body and its workings or on medicine as it is understood today. Instead, trephination was done to let out the evil spirits that early people thought caused disease. The body's anatomy (the way it is formed) and its physiology (the way it works) were mysteries that prehistoric people faced with the aid of magic and religion, not science.

But even unscientific practices like trephination must have taught these prehistoric humans some facts about the body. They must have learned, for instance, that the skull is made of bone, that the flesh contains blood, and that inside the skull is a soft, grayish material: the brain. Over a period of centuries, small bits of knowledge were gained by such observations, but understanding remained almost nonexistent.

Nearly 3,000 years ago, the ancient Egyptians also gathered facts through the practice of their religion, as they attempted to foretell the future by a process called *divining*, which involved examining the inner organs of animals. The Egyptians also preserved the bodies of their dead with a method called *embalming*, which required opening up the body and removing the inner organs. The bodies were then filled with strong spices and other materials that kept them from decomposing. Thus the Egyptians learned much about the appearance of both human and animal organs and discovered in a general way how such organs were arranged inside the body.

It was the Greeks, however, who first deliberately investigated the subject of anatomy. In the 5th century B.C., the Greek physician Hippocrates (c.460–377 B.C.) was among the first to suggest that the body's parts were interrelated and that illness occurred when a specific part malfunctioned.

A century later, the philosopher Aristotle (384–322 B.C.) founded the science of comparative anatomy by dissecting animals (cutting them apart for study) and comparing their organs. Aristotle described arteries, veins, and the digestive organs, among many other internal parts. But like those who had gone before him, he did not understand much about how these structures worked, believing, for example, that the heart was the organ of thinking and that the brain worked only to cool the heart.

By the 2nd century A.D., the Greek scientist Galen (129–c.199) was dissecting the bodies of hogs and apes and recording his findings. Although he did not dissect human beings, Galen assumed that human organs were like those of other animals. For lack of better knowledge, other scientists believed and accepted Galen's theories about human anatomy for 1,200 years. In fact, until nearly the end of the Middle Ages (a period roughly extending from the 6th to the 15th century), Euro-

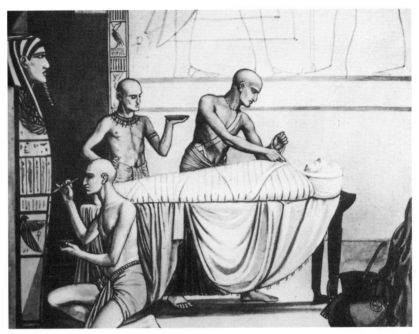

Ancient Egyptians used a method called embalming to preserve the bodies of their dead. This process involved removing the internal organs and filling the body with strong spices that kept it from decaying.

pean physicians and scientists depended almost entirely on Galen's writings for their knowledge of the human body.

It may seem strange that the science of anatomy did not progress much over those 1,200 years, but this lack of advancement was no accident. The early Christian church banned the practice of dissecting human bodies, so there was no way for scientists to learn more about human anatomy. During that time, most medical knowledge was passed on by Christian monks, who were usually more concerned with relieving suffering than discovering new information. Also, Galen was still so famous that few dared contradict his ancient teachings. "It is better to be wrong with Galen than to be right with others," went a saying of the age.

But during the Renaissance in Europe (a period that lasted approximately from the 14th to the 17th century) people began, once again, to seek out knowledge for its own sake. At the same time, artists began studying the human body closely, in order to paint, draw, and sculpt it more correctly. The Italian artist and scientist Leonardo da Vinci (1452–1519) performed many dissections of human bodies and drew

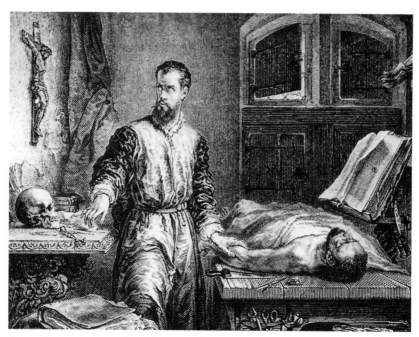

Sixteenth-century anatomist Andreas Vesalius was among the first to perform autopsies of the human body. These examinations enabled him to provide accurate descriptions of such bodily functions as circulation.

accurate pictures of the heart, muscles, blood vessels, and unborn infants. Based on his own observations Leonardo was the first to realize that air does not move directly from tubes in the lungs into the blood, as others then thought it did.

An even greater student of anatomy was the Belgian Andreas Vesalius (1514–64). At the University of Padua, where he was appointed a professor at age 24, Vesalius performed the most thorough, accurate examinations of the human body that had ever been done. Then, at the age of 29, he published his great book, *De humani corporis fabrica* (On the anatomy of the human body), which is still considered an accurate description of bones, muscles, veins, and nerves as well as of the heart, brain, and other organs.

Less than a century later, another important anatomist, Fabricius, taught at the University of Padua. Fabricius (1537–1619) studied the valves in the veins—tiny flaps that keep blood moving toward the heart and prevent it from backing up. When the Englishman William Harvey (1578–1657) went to Padua to become a doctor, he studied with Fabricius and learned about the valves. Returning to London, Harvey worked for 20 years to find out more about them and about how the blood moves in the body. At last, in 1628, Harvey published his revolutionary findings in his book *De motu cordis et sanguinis* (Concerning the motion of the heart and blood). Harvey showed that instead of making new blood for each heartbeat, as had been thought previously, the heart pumps the same blood around the body again and again.

Because the microscope was not yet perfected (invented in 1609, the microscope was a by-product of Galileo Galilei's invention of the telescope), Harvey could not find the precise spot where the blood ceased moving away from the heart and began moving back toward it. But in 1650 a way to see clearly through the microscope was developed, and in 1661 the Italian scientist Marcello Malpighi (1628–94) was able to see tiny vessels called *capillaries* as he examined a frog's lung. Only one-tenth the width of a human hair, the capillaries link arteries (vessels that carry blood away from the heart) to veins (vessels that move blood back to the heart). Thus, Malpighi found the last link in the circulatory system.

Malpighi's contemporary was the Dutch scientist and microscope pioneer Antonie van Leeuwenhoek (1632–1723). An amateur scientist who made his living as a draper (a dealer in cloth), Leeuwenhoek built the most powerful microscopes of his time—some of which magnified objects 270 times. With his advanced instruments Leeuwenhoek was able to describe muscle fibers and other microscopic structures of the human body in great detail. He was also the first to see and describe bacteria, tiny one-celled organisms whose existence was unknown before that time.

Another skilled amateur was the British clergyman Stephen Hales (1677–1761), who discovered a way to directly measure blood pressure. By connecting tall glass tubes filled with mercury to the large blood vessels of horses, Hales was able to see when the animals' blood pressure changed. A change in blood pressure forced the mercury in the tubes to move up or down. Hales's work laid the foundations for modern understanding of fluid pressures in the body. Also in the 17th century, the British scientist Robert Boyle (1627–1691) showed that breathing moves oxygen into the body, that the oxygen turns blood cells bright red, and that most life processes rely on the use of oxygen to create energy.

The 18th century was an era of rapid advances in all areas of knowledge about the body. The Italian scientist Abbate Sallanzani (1729–99) discovered that the stomach produced gastric juices that helped dissolve food. Soon after that, in America, the surgeon William Beaumont (1785–1853) met a trapper who had been shot in the stomach. The

Dutch scientist Antonie van Leeuwenhoek built the most powerful microscopes of his time. With these instruments he was able to describe muscle fibers and other microscopic structures of the human body in great detail.

man survived, but with a permanent hole in his side; through this hole, called a *fistula*, the man's stomach could be seen. With this man's cooperation, Beaumont was able to obtain gastric juices, time their flow, and study the movements of the stomach in great detail.

Around the same time of Beaumont's experiments, Luigi Galvani of Bologna (1737–98) showed that electricity caused nerves to stimulate muscles, while the Swiss scientist Albrecht von Haller (1708–77) learned that these electrical impulses are carried to the nerves by the spinal cord. During this same era in France, the chemist Antoine-Laurent Lavoisier (1743–94) was pioneering in the study of metabolism; that is, he was learning how the body burns food, with the aid of oxygen, to produce energy.

In Great Britain, interest in human anatomy was so widespread at this time that scientists had trouble getting enough bodies to dissect. This was because only the bodies of hanged criminals could legally be used for study. To satisfy the need, there arose the ghoulish group of criminals known as resurrection men and resurrection women who, for a fee, robbed graves and delivered fresh bodies to scientists for secret dissection. In a few cases people were even murdered to get bodies for sale to dissectors. Finally, in 1831 the British Parliament passed the Anatomy Act, which said that unclaimed bodies from morgues (the places where bodies are kept before burial) could be given to scientists. Thus ended the horrid era of grave robbing for scientific purposes.

The 19th century was a time of even greater progress for scientists studying the workings of the human body. Indeed, the 1800s saw the identification of the cell as the basic building block of life, the discovery of the ways in which substances pass through membranes, and knowledge of the way the body maintains a balance of chemicals and water.

The French chemist Louis Pasteur (1822–95) established the germ theory of disease and developed the method of heating liquids, such as milk, to kill microscopic organisms that spoil them. This process, known as pasteurization, is still used today. Pasteur was also one of the first scientists to develop and successfully use a vaccine. This vaccine, for hydrophobia (rabies), involved injecting the patient with increasingly strong doses of the rabies virus to build up immunity. Pasteur's first patient, a young boy bitten by a rabid dog, was given the vaccination and survived.

Scientists continued to make new breakthroughs in the 20th century. The discovery of different blood types; of the tiny substructures inside cells; of the structure and function of the inner ear; of the way muscles contract and relax; of the structure of DNA (the genetic material by which living organisms pass on traits to offspring); and of the way pain is produced and transmitted have revealed information about the body that would have amazed scientists who lived just a century ago.

Even so, the search to find out more about the body goes on, for no matter how much is known, it seems that more always remains to be learned. The immune system, for example—the body's way of defending itself against infection—is only beginning to be understood. Scientists continue to study the reproductive system, especially its ability to pass inherited traits from one generation to the next. The nervous system, particularly the brain, remains more an uncharted frontier than an understood territory. And almost every other part of the body also offers further opportunities for examination—and poses questions that still need answers.

What is known about the body provides the basis for many other areas of study: those related to surgery and to medicines for treating many illnesses and injuries, for example. Future discoveries may provide even better treatments. They may help us live longer, cure presently incurable diseases, or remedy disabilities such as blindness or mental retardation, to mention just a few of the possibilities.

But knowledge of the body is not only for doctors and scientists. A basic understanding of how the body functions is one of the best tools all kinds of people can use to keep their own bodies healthy and working well. After all, by knowing what a thing is made of and how it works, people can better understand how to take care of it.

2

THE NERVOUS SYSTEM

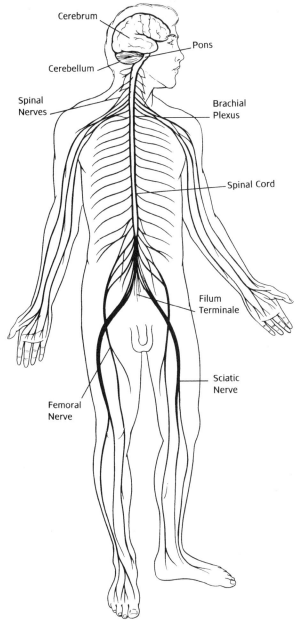

Cerebrum

Pons

Cerebellum

Spinal
Nerves

Brachial
Plexus

Spinal Cord

Filum
Terminale

Sciatic
Nerve

Femoral
Nerve

Every moment throughout its lifetime, the human body is performing hundreds of functions. Some are deliberate, such as eating, walking, or talking. Others are automatic, such as breathing, sleeping, digesting food, or circulating blood. Many are related to or dependent upon one another: the faster a person walks, for instance, the faster he or she breathes—automatically—to supply oxygen for the increased work. At the same time, the walker may be planning a job interview, worrying about an upcoming school examination, listening to a favorite song on a portable radio—or all of these things at once.

How can the body organize so many different functions so rapidly and with so few mistakes? The answer lies in the body's complex information and communication network: the nervous system. The nervous system consists of the brain and spinal cord (the central nervous system) and a branching network of nerves throughout the body (the peripheral nervous system). Along this vast network travel two kinds of messages: *afferent messages,* which send information about the outside world and the body to the brain; and *efferent messages,* which deliver instructions from the brain to the body. Both types of message are transmitted via nerves.

Nerves themselves are cells—the basic building blocks from which all living matter is made. But they are special cells, linked to one another by tiny branchlike structures called *axons* and *dendrites.* Each nerve cell has a cell body; many dendrites, which function as message receivers; and a single long axon, which sends messages. At the axon's end are tiny bumps called *telodendrons.* Surrounding most nerve cells are cells called *glia;* coated with a fatty substance called *myelin,* the glia insulate nerve cells from one another. The only parts of nerve cells not covered by glia are the area adjacent to tiny gaps—*synapses*—that lie between the axon of one nerve cell and the dendrites of the next.

The actual message-sending process works this way: when a nerve cell (or *neuron*) is at rest, it contains negatively charged potassium *ions* (ions are atoms, groups of atoms, or subatomic particles that carry an electrical force). At the same time, fluid outside the neuron holds sodium ions carrying a positive charge. When a neuron sends a nerve impulse, it first fires off a burst of chemicals called *neurotransmitters* from its axon. These chemicals flow across the synapse and lock onto receptor sites on the receiving neuron's dendrites—a process that takes less than one-thousandth of a second.

In the receiving cell, the neurotransmitters cause negative potassium ions to leak out and positive sodium ions to leak in. In response, the receiver neuron forces out the positive ions and takes negative ions in

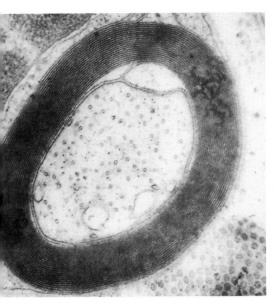

An electronmicrograph of a myelin sheath magnified 30,000 times. The myelin sheath (shown here as dark rings around the nerve cell) is really a fatty substance that coats the glia, the cell's supporting tissue.

again, to restore its normal negative interior. This positive-negative flip-flop process moves through the neuron and out along its axon to the telodendrons. There, tiny sacs called *synaptic vesicles* burst open, releasing more neurotransmitters—which jump the next synapse, find the next neuron's dendrites, and begin the whole process all over again. It is this ability of neurons to transmit nerve impulses—chemically between nerve cells, electrically when inside them—that links the brain with the body and the outside world.

The central coordinator of all this message sending and message receiving is the brain. Weighing about three pounds in an adult, it is made of up two kinds of tissue: gray matter, which consists of nerve-cell bodies, and white matter, which consists of the axons, dendrites, and glia. The brain is divided into three main parts, the largest of which is the *forebrain.* This section, with its gray, deeply grooved surface, is the part of the brain most people know from pictures. The forebrain is divided into halves, the right and left *cerebral hemispheres,* linked by a ribbon of connecting fibers called the *corpus callosum.*

The grooved surface of the forebrain, about ¼ inch thick and covering both hemispheres, is called the *cerebral cortex.* Flattened out, it would measure about 2 ½ square feet. The cerebral cortex is made up of about 10 billion cells and is divided into four lobes, each having its own responsibilities for organizing thought, sensation, and movement.

The *frontal lobes,* responsible for complex thoughts, decisions, and judgments concerning right and wrong, are located just behind the forehead bone. From the frontal lobes also come messages that tell the body's muscles when and how to move. Behind the frontal lobes are the *parietal lobes,* where some information from the senses is processed. Below the parietal lobes lie the *temporal lobes,* where among other things the speech center is located; here the brain makes sense of written or spoken language. Finally, at the back of the skull lie the *occipital lobes,* where information from the eyes is processed. In addition to these areas for which the functions are known, there are many parts of the cerebral cortex that have not yet had their specific functions identified.

Below the frontal lobes lies the second main part of the brain, the *midbrain.* The midbrain contains the *hypothalamus,* which produces hormones that control growth, temperature, and water balances in the body and activate sexual behavior. The *substantia nigra* also lies here; it is the part of the brain responsible for producing the chemical *dopamine*—a substance that regulates muscle rigidity and prevents muscles from trembling.

Axons and dendrites serve as the essential link that allows neurons to communicate with each other. Nerve messages are received through the dendrites and transmitted along the axon.

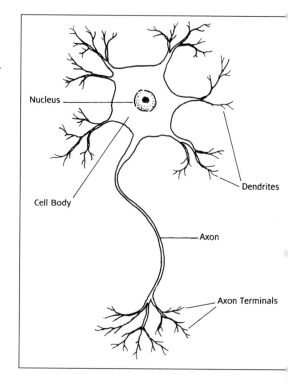

Nucleus

Cell Body

Dendrites

Axon

Axon Terminals

Below the midbrain lies the *hindbrain,* which itself has three parts: the *medulla oblongata,* a bulb at the spinal cord's top; the *cerebellum,* shaped like two linked spheres; and the *pons,* a ridgelike bridge connecting the two spheres of the cerebellum. The hindbrain is the center of control over the body's most basic functions, such as regulating heartbeat, breathing, blood pressure, and other vital activities.

Between the brain and the bones of the skull lie three protective membranes. The outer one is the tough, leathery *dura mater;* next is the *arachnoid,* and finally the *pia mater,* which lies very closely against the surface of the brain itself. Also, in four hollow spaces within the brain called *ventricles,* a special liquid, *cerebrospinal fluid,* moistens and cushions the brain.

Messages between the brain and other parts of the head move via 12 pairs of main nerves called *cranial nerves,* whose roots lie directly in the brain. The 12 pairs of cranial nerves are responsible for eye movement; for sensation in the face, jaws, and teeth; for face movements; for hearing and balance; for the sense of taste; for swallowing; and for the movement of the tongue. The 10th pair of cranial nerves, called the *vagus nerves,* are the only cranial nerves that extend into the lower body; these very complex nerves control movements of the voice box, or *larynx* (the organ responsible for sound and speech), along with vitally important functions of the heart, lungs, stomach, and other organs.

Messages between the brain and the rest of the body move via 31 pairs of nerves branching off the spinal cord. This main highway for brain-body communication is a cable of nerve tissue about 18 inches long, running from the base of the brain down the middle of the back, inside the bones of the spinal column. Like the brain, it is bathed in cerebrospinal fluid, which cushions and moistens it; also like the brain, it contains both white matter and gray matter. Once the main spinal nerves have branched off the spinal cord, they branch again and again in a network that reaches every area of the body. This branching network of nerves lying outside the brain and spinal cord composes the peripheral nervous system, keeping the whole body in constant communication with the brain.

Many of the signals that the brain sends to the body are the result of conscious deliberation—such as the signal to raise one's arms. As we mentioned above, however, some bodily activities are automatic and are controlled by the brain without one's being aware of them. Automatic functions such as breathing, digesting, maintaining blood pressure, and regulating heartbeat are directed by two special subgroups of

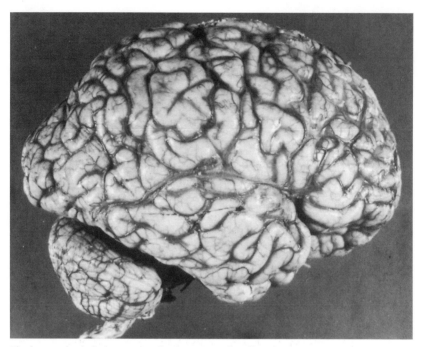

The human brain is the communications center for all nerve messages.

nerves that make up the sympathetic and parasympathetic nervous systems (both systems are actually subdivisions of the autonomic nervous system). Both carry messages from the brain to the body, but they are not under the brain's conscious control; rather, they may be stimulated by emotions and cause the body to react physically to feelings such as fear, anger, or calmness.

When a person is startled, angry, tense, or under some other emotional stress, the brain automatically begins sending messages to the sympathetic nerves. In essence, the messages tell the body to get ready to cope with an unpleasant situation. They cause the *adrenal glands* to give off *adrenaline,* or *epinephrine,* a substance that raises the heart rate and blood pressure, shunts extra blood to the limbs, increases sweating, and prepares the body to meet the emergency the brain has perceived.

By contrast, when the brain perceives that no danger exists, that the body is well fed, and that life in general is safe and pleasant, it sends signals to the parasympathetic nerves. These nerves tell the body to relax by causing the release of a substance called *acetylcholine.* Under these circumstances, acetylcholine slows the heart rate, relaxes the blood vessels, and increases such "peacetime" body functions as digestion and glandular activity.

One type of nervous system message not under the brain's conscious control is the sensory nerve message. One does not decide to see, hear, taste, or feel, for example; one does it automatically. Sensory information enters the nervous system via special nerve endings in the skin and other sense organs. In the skin, for instance, the nerve endings can be stimulated by pressure, temperature change, or vibration. Sensory messages travel up the network of the peripheral nervous system to sense-input collection centers called *ganglia*—knobby groups of nerve cell bodies, most often on the outside of the brain or spinal cord. Ganglionic nerve fibers send the information up the spinal cord to the brain. Pain is a special kind of sensory message that occurs when the body malfunctions or suffers injury. When pain-sensitive nerve endings called *nociceptors* are stimulated—by the heat from a flame, the prick of a pin, or any number of other pain-causing stimuli—they send information about the injury to the brain. It is in the brain that pain is actually recognized and experienced. At once, the brain begins sending instructions to the body, ordering it to remedy the pain-causing problem. At the same time it processes the pain message further, deciding more about what kind of pain is occurring; evaluating how serious the pain-causing situation may be; generating emotions of fear, sadness, or anger; and storing memories of the pain and what caused it in order to avoid it in the future. The brain also releases substances called *enkephalins,* natural pain-relief chemicals that work to block more pain messages.

Finally, of course, some nerve messages are under the brain's deliberate control. These consist primarily of motor nerve messages: the directions the brain sends to *voluntary muscles*—the ones the brain moves on purpose—to make them contract. Messages travel along motor nerves in the same way that other nerve impulses travel—by a chain of tiny electrochemical bursts over the gaps between nerve fibers. Once the messages reach a muscle, however, one more gap must be jumped: the tiny space between the final nerve fiber and the muscle itself. To bridge this gap, certain neurons have end plates very near the surface of muscle cells. When a motor nerve end fires, it gives off acetylcholine. This substance triggers the muscle cell's eventual contraction, causing movement.

Scientists are only now beginning to understand the more complex and mysterious aspects of the central and peripheral nervous systems. It is not yet clear, for example, just how the brain stores and retrieves information, how it processes language, or how the brain's many sub-systems are organized to maintain consciousness. For all of its complexity and mystery, however, the brain is still part of the body, and discoveries about the body's other systems invariably shed light on the workings of the brain. One such system—the sensory system—is of particular interest to neurophysiologists, the scientists who are trying to unlock the brain's secrets. But like the brain, the sensory system holds mysteries of its own.

3

THE SENSES

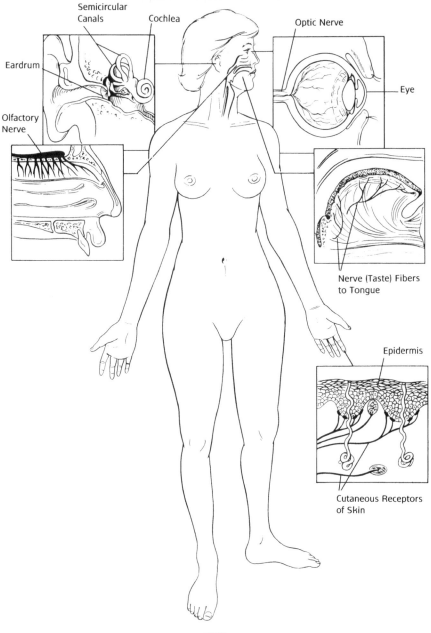

Semicircular Canals

Cochlea

Optic Nerve

Eardrum

Eye

Olfactory Nerve

Nerve (Taste) Fibers to Tongue

Epidermis

Cutaneous Receptors of Skin

The five senses—sight, hearing, smell, taste, and touch—are made possible by the body's information-gathering equipment. The senses provide essential information about the world—the location of food and water, for instance—as well as the experiences that make life rich: the smell of roses, the pounding of ocean waves, the taste of ice cream, or the touch of a loved one's hand and the sight of his or her face.

Sense impressions are received through the sense organs: the eyes, ears, nose, tongue, and skin. Each of these organs gathers a special kind of information. The eyes, for instance, are sensitive to light, whereas the ears respond to vibrations in the air. Each sensory organ sends its own kind of information through the nervous system to the brain, which in turn interprets the input; a pattern of light and shadow may be interpreted as the face of a friend, while touches on the skin may indicate that a towel is too rough. Together, sensory impressions are what give humans their perceptions of the physical world.

THE SENSE OF SMELL

Compared with that of other creatures, the human sense of smell is weak. Silkworm moths, for instance, can smell mates at a distance of miles, and pigs can smell truffles (a mushroomlike food) buried six inches underground; bloodhounds may follow the scent of their quarry even after two days of heavy rain. None of these feats are possible for human beings.

Part of the reason for the shortcomings in humans' sense of smell lies in the way humans evolved. When the ancestors of *Homo sapiens* moved out of the ocean, onto land, and then into the trees, the senses of sight and hearing became more important to survival than the sense of smell. By the time prehumans descended to solid ground again, the brain had adapted. Its sight and hearing centers had grown larger, while the olfactory (smelling) center had shrunk. In modern humans, many of the brain's original olfactory structures have merged with the *limbic system,* the center responsible for human emotions. This is why a familiar smell can bring back vivid feelings and memories.

The physical sensations of smelling are based on two facts. First, molecules of most materials are released into the air. Second, tissue inside the nose is rich in nerve endings that are not only stimulated by molecules but can differentiate between them as well. When a person

Perfume testers test each new fragrance before it is manufactured. In humans, many of the olfactory structures have merged with the limbic system, the center responsible for emotions. This is why a particular scent, for example, can evoke vivid feelings.

breathes in such molecules, they reach an area of tissue deep in each nostril called the *olfactory area*. This region is made up of skin covered by a thin layer of watery material called *mucus*. In the mucus, thousands of microscopically tiny hairs wave back and forth. The hairs are fibers of the first cranial nerve, which is responsible for sending smell messages to the brain. The hairs send their messages to the brain's smell interpretation center—part of the cerebral cortex. The brain interprets the messages as sweet, acid, rancid, burnt, or a combination of these. The exact interpretation depends on the size and shape of molecules stimulating the nose's olfactory area.

THE SENSE OF TASTE

Like the sense of smell, the sense of taste is stimulated by the molecules released by various substances. Nerve endings that take in taste sensations are located on the tongue, in the taste buds. They lie in the grooves between the *papillae* (tiny swellings that give the tongue its spongy appearance).

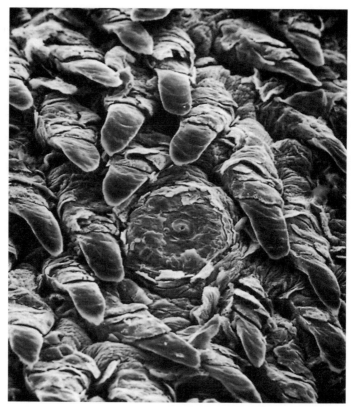

An electron micrograph of a taste bud. Each bud contains nerve endings that receive and process taste sensations.

One taste bud contains about a dozen taste cells, each about four-thousandths of an inch long, packed into the bud like the petals of an unopened flower. At each bud's top end is a *pore:* an opening to the tongue's surface. Poking up through the opening are tiny hairs called *taste hairs.* At the bud's base lie nerve fibers that carry taste information through the nervous system to the brain. When food is chewed, some molecules of it dissolve in *saliva* (fluid made by glands under the tongue called *salivary glands*). The saliva then carries the molecules to the tiny hairs in the pores of the taste buds. Stimulated by the molecules, the hairs send signals down through the taste cells to the nerve fibers at their base.

From there, the signals travel to one of two nerves: the *lingual nerve* from the front and middle of the tongue, or one of the pair of *glos-*

sopharyngeal nerves from the back of the tongue. Both send information to an area of the brain called the *somesthetic band,* where the taste interpretation center is located. When the signals reach this band the brain interprets them and generates the experience of a particular taste.

All taste buds do not detect the same kinds of tastes. Buds at the tip of the tongue detect sweetness and saltiness, whereas the buds on the tongue's sides taste mostly sourness, and buds at the back of the tongue are best at sensing bitterness. Thus a salt grain on the back of the tongue will not be tasted very much until saliva carries some salt molecules to the tip, where salt-sensitive taste buds are. Likewise a small amount of lemon juice on the tip of the tongue will not be tasted much until it reaches the sour-sensing taste buds.

Scientists do not yet know why different taste buds are sensitive to different tastes. It is also unclear just how taste cells are stimulated by contact with molecules of food or other material. And although these scientists do know that the texture and temperature of foods

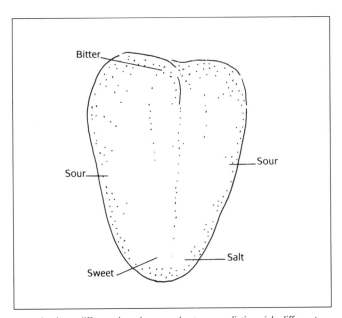

Taste buds at different locations on the tongue distinguish different types of flavors: those at the tip of the tongue detect sweetness and saltiness; those at the back detect bitterness; and those along the sides detect sourness.

contribute to their taste—for instance, a cold slice of tough roast beef does not taste as good as a hot, tender one—they do not yet know why this is so. It is known that taste bud nerve fibers may branch out to nearby pressure- or temperature-sensitive nerves, but how these nerves affect one another has not yet been discovered. Humans know from experience, too, that the appearance of food—whether it looks good—affects the way it tastes, but this relationship awaits explanation as well. Finally, the way foods smell is very important to the way they taste. Many people, for example, lose their appetite when they have a cold because they cannot smell food and therefore cannot taste it very well, either. Why this is so is not clear, but certain facts suggest possible reasons. First, in early vertebrates (creatures with spines) the olfactory sense was a main way of finding food; thus the sense of smell has been linked with food for millions of years. Also, the sense of smell in modern humans affects areas of the brain from the hypothalamus (which controls appetite and pleasure) to the limbic system (concerned with emotions) to the brain stem (controlling the most basic functions of life). Because all of these areas have some effect on the vital function of eating, it is easy to see how senses of taste and smell might reasonably be related—although, again, just how is not yet known.

The sense of taste is important to nutrition; the pleasure of eating makes the digestive system work better. This was first suggested in 1895, after a nine-year-old New York boy (known only as Tom) accidentally gulped down a mouthful of boiling hot soup. Scars from the burn closed off his *esophagus,* the tube that carries food from the mouth to the stomach. Doctors inserted a tube directly into his stomach so that he would not starve; he "ate" by pouring liquefied foods down the tube. But even though the food he took in this way was nourishing, he could not gain weight and he always felt hungry. Nothing seemed to solve this problem, until the boy himself began taking tastes of his food before pouring it into the feeding tube. After he began tasting meals—even though he was not swallowing them in the normal way—he gained weight, his hunger went away, and he was able to thrive.

Studies by Dr. Henry Janowitz and Franklin Hollander at Mt. Sinai Hospital in New York show that when people enjoy the taste of foods the stomach makes twice as much digestive juice, the juices flow three times as quickly, and the body digests food for two hours longer than when people eat meals they do not enjoy. Thus a balanced diet that tastes good is apparently better for a person than the same diet less tastefully prepared.

THE SENSE OF SIGHT

Unlike the senses of smell and taste, which are stimulated by chemical molecules, the sense of sight is stimulated by energy—the energy of light—and it is extremely powerful. It has been estimated that the human visual system contains an amazing 70% of all the sensory nerve endings in the body. One nerve fiber serves every 2 muscles of the eye, compared to 1 for every 200 muscles in the rest of the body. And the *optic nerves*—the tracts that carry sight messages to the brain—have as many fibers as all the nerves serving all the voluntary muscles of the body combined. Thus humans can see both near and far-off objects, in light or near darkness and in a wide variety of colors, and can follow

The sense of sight, which is stimulated by light, is very powerful. This is why human beings can see both near and far-off objects and can differentiate between a wide variety of colors.

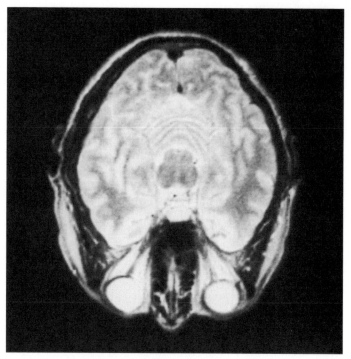

An MRI (magnetic resonance imaging) of the human skull, showing the brain, eyeballs, and optic nerves.

moving objects, estimate distances, and distinguish between the edges of very complex physical objects.

The eye itself is a globe of tissue resting in the protective bony eye socket. Many of its parts serve as a support system: muscles that help the eye hold its shape; the *conjunctiva* that moisten and protect it; fluids called humors that are found in the eyeball; the *sclera* (the outer skin of the eye's white part); and blood vessels that nourish the eye.

The parts of the eye that see (sense light, process it, and send messages to the brain) are, from front to back: the *cornea*, the *iris*, the *lens* with the *ciliary muscles* and *zonula ciliaris* holding it in place, the *retina*, and at the very rear of the eye, the *optic nerve* leading to the brain. For proper vision, a clear image must be transmitted to the retina and the image must be sent to the brain.

The process of seeing an object or person is very complex and involves a number of different steps before the object or person is really seen. Still, the human body is such an amazing machine that the entire process takes only thousandths of a second to complete. Light rays first pass through the cornea, the clear covering on the front of the eyeball. Next, they pass through the *pupil*—the dark spot in the eye's center. The pupil is simply a hole that lets light into the eye. It can enlarge to let more light in or contract to keep excess light out. Pupil size is controlled automatically by muscles around the *iris* (the eye's colored part).

Next, light reaches the *lens,* a clear solid structure held up by tiny fibers called zonula fibers, stretched between the lens and the ciliary body. The lens bends rays of light so that they strike the retina perfectly and produce a clear image on it. The lens does this by changing its shape when the zonula fibers tighten or loosen, in response to instructions from the brain. Changing the lens shape (a change called *accommodation)* bends the light rays either more or less—focusing the image of objects that are near or far away. Then the focused rays of light pass through the clear fluid of the *vitreous humor,* the liquid inside the eyeball, and land on the retina.

In the retina two different types of special light-receiving cells are found—*rods* and *cones.* Cones are packed at the center of the retina, called the *macula.* They handle sharp, straight-ahead vision. Each cone has a nerve fiber connecting it to the brain via the optic nerve—the main sight nerve. The macular area is so important that even though it is only 1% of the retina, its nerves make up over half the fibers in the optic nerve.

Cones are also responsible for color vision because they not only respond to light but can pick out different wavelengths of light. A person sees a red fire truck as red, for instance, because the light bouncing off the truck into the eye is light of a certain wavelength. To understand wavelengths, think of a ray of light as a wavy line. A line with a lot of waves packed into it has a short wavelength. A line with fewer waves—more length between one wave and the next—has a long wavelength. Light waves of different lengths are seen as different colors because they stimulate different chemicals, called pigments, in the retina's cones.

The rest of the retina—the nonmacular part—sees things in all directions other than straight ahead. This capability, known as peripheral vision, is handled by the rod cells. Rod cells are not located in the retina's center but are scattered everywhere outside of it. They do not produce as sharp a picture because they do not each have nerve fibers of their own. They also do not see colors as well as cones do. But rods are better than cones at distinguishing movement of objects not directly ahead and are better at distinguishing objects in dim light.

Once the retina gathers and focuses light and has stimulated the roughly 100 million rods and 6 or 7 million cones there, the rods and cones produce tiny nerve impulses. These pass through nerve fibers to the optic nerve, which carries them to the brain's *optic chiasma,* the place where the optic nerves cross one another. At this crossing, the signals switch: signals from the left eye travel to the vision center in the right parietal lobe and signals from the right eye, to the left parietal lobe. Finally, the last step in the process of sight occurs: the brain takes all the vision signals and meshes them to give a single picture from the two eyes. This processing of visual signals takes place in the occipital lobes—the rear part of the brain—where several nerve layers refine the incoming information from the eyes into the final image that the conscious person perceives. The first nerve layer passes on millions of bits of information about edges, textures, and colors; after much processing by the layers in between, the final nerve layer passes on a message that the frontal lobe of the brain—the conscious part—can understand. In this way, what began as millions of separate messages about light energy becomes one message: *this is a tree,* or *this is a chair,* or whatever the eyes are focused on. So far, no computer on earth can perform this feat as well as the human visual system can.

THE SENSE OF HEARING

The sense of hearing gathers information from vibrations in liquids, solids, or gases. When these vibrations strike the human eardrum, they are heard as sound. The vibrations themselves—sound waves—travel through air or other matter in the same way as ripples spread from a stone tossed into a pool of water: outward at a constant speed in all directions. Like light waves, sound waves have length. Also like light waves, they have frequency, the number of sound waves produced per second. The higher the vibration's frequency, the higher pitched the sound. A sound wave also has intensity—a measurement of how *much* energy it has—which is heard as the sound's loudness. And it has tones—separate vibrations within its main vibration. The tone of a sound wave may be compared to tiny wavelets within the main ripple

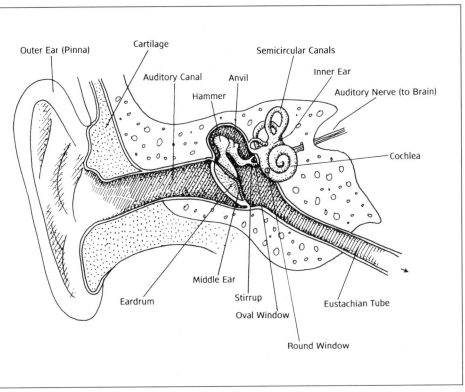

Outer Ear (Pinna)

Cartilage

Auditory Canal

Anvil

Hammer

Semicircular Canals

Inner Ear

Auditory Nerve (to Brain)

Cochlea

Middle Ear

Eardrum

Stirrup

Oval Window

Eustachian Tube

Round Window

The sense of hearing is the result of air-pressure variations that are routed to the cochlea and are then translated into patterns of neural activity.

spreading across a pool. Tone is the quality that makes a note played on a guitar sound different from the same note played on a piano.

The ear is the organ that senses sound vibrations, transforms them into nerve messages, and sends the messages along the auditory nerve to the brain. It has three parts: the outer, middle, and inner ear. The outer ear is the flap of skin and cartilage, what most people think of as the ear itself, and is shaped somewhat like a horn to gather sound vibrations. The vibrations pass into the ear canal, the hole leading from the outside of the skull to the inside. This canal is lined with skin bearing tiny hairs, along with sweat glands that make *cerumen* (commonly known as earwax). The whole outer structure is designed to keep out foreign matter, such as dirt or insects. It also concentrates sound waves and aims them directly at the *tympanic membrane*—the eardrum.

The eardrum is like the top of a drum: round, taut, stiff, and able to vibrate. When sound waves strike the eardrum, it moves only about a half-billionth of an inch, but this movement is enough to send signals through nerve fibers to the middle ear, which is richly supplied with more nerve fibers to transmit sound vibrations even further inward. No larger than a pea, the middle ear holds three small bones: the *hammer*, the *anvil*, and the *stirrup*. The roof of the middle ear is a thin bone dividing it from the brain; its floor divides it from major arteries in the neck. At its back an opening leads to bones of the skull called the *mastoid process*. Another opening leads to the *eustachian tube*, which connects the ear to the back of the throat.

Within the middle ear, sound vibrations multiply a hundredfold. One can see how this can happen by thinking of a long stick lying over the top of a rock. The short end of the stick is in one's hand; the long end sticks out over the rock. When one pushes down a little on the short end, the long end rises high into the air. In the same way sound is amplified (made stronger) a hundredfold when sound vibrations press on the short bone of the middle ear (the hammer handle) thus moving the long bone (the anvil) a proportionately greater distance.

At the inner portion of the middle ear lies an oval window made of a thin membrane (skinlike structure). Beyond it, in the inner ear, lies a closed tube filled with fluid. When amplified sound waves from the middle ear press against the oval window, the fluid in the tube of the inner ear is compressed. This compression transmits pressure to the tiny hairs at the tube's innermost end, in an area known as the *organ of Corti*. From the 17,000 cells of this organ, the hairs—actually fibers of the acoustic nerve—become stimulated and begin sending messages to the main body of the nerve. Along these 30,000 nerve fibers, the sound messages travel to the *auditory cortex*—the area of the brain that experiences and interprets sound.

THE SENSE OF TOUCH

The sense of touch brings information to the brain through the skin. The average thickness of the skin is $\frac{1}{20}$ of an inch, yet all of it is generously studded with nerve endings—up to 1,300 per square inch. These nerve endings fall into two categories: capsulelike bodies and free endings resembling a network of lace. The capsules are mostly responsible

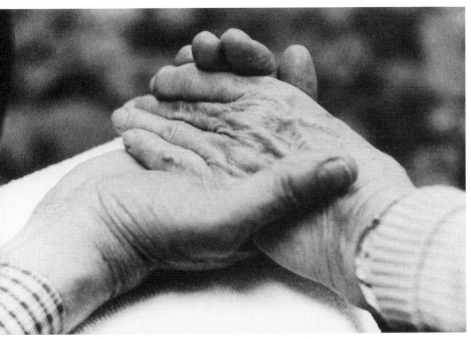

The sense of touch provides a person with a sense of where his or her body ends and the rest of the world begins.

for information about sense-of-touch messages within the body: in joints, organs, and blood vessels, for instance. The free endings are more concerned with gathering information from outside the body—for instance, from the surface of the skin.

Both kinds of nerve endings are sensitive to heat, cold, contact, pressure, and pain. But these five types of touch sensitivity may combine to produce a myriad of different sensory impressions, such as dampness, hardness, roughness or smoothness, largeness or smallness. The lips, tongue, and the tip of the nose are some of the most sensitive areas of the body to touch sensations from the outer world; after these areas, the fingertips are the most sensitive—twice as sensitive as other parts of the hand. Hair-covered skin is particularly sensitive; nerves around some hair roots can be stimulated by moving the hair as little as four-billionths of an inch.

Once stimulated, nerve endings for the sense of touch send their messages to the spinal cord, which relays them to the brain. At this point the cerebral cortex interprets and makes sense of these messages. As with the other senses, many facts about this particular process are not yet clear to scientists. It is not yet clear whether messages from pain-sensitive nerve endings are processed by the brain the same way that the brain processes nonpainful sensory messages.

In addition to providing information about what is happening to the body, the sense of touch provides a sense of where the body ends and the outer world begins—giving a sense of self. Using messages from the sense of touch all over the body, the brain builds a mental picture of the body as a whole—a physical sense of self that enables humans to determine where their bodies end and the outside world begins.

Thus, all senses—taste, smell, sight, hearing, and touch—help humans recognize and manage a vital relationship: that between the human body and the complex world in which it lives.

4

THE RESPIRATORY SYSTEM

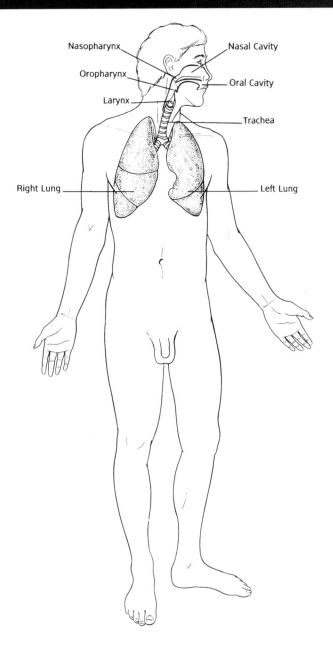

Nasopharynx

Nasal Cavity

Oropharynx

Oral Cavity

Larynx

Trachea

Right Lung

Left Lung

The human body can survive for weeks without food and for days without water but only for about three minutes without air. This is because the body's cells depend upon the existence of oxygen at every moment. Take oxygen away, and one of the body's crucial processes—metabolism—cannot take place.

Metabolism is the process of chemical change living cells must constantly undergo in order to supply energy to themselves. One can think of metabolism as a tiny fire, constantly burning fuel (food), giving off heat (energy), and creating ashes (waste). Like a fire, metabolism in a living cell consumes oxygen as it turns fuel to energy; without oxygen the fires of metabolism—and the cell itself—would die. Similarly, cells die if waste products of metabolism are not removed, much as a fire can be smothered by its own ashes. Thus living cells must constantly receive oxygen and must constantly excrete carbon dioxide. This process is called respiration.

Oxygen travels from the air to the lungs by inhalation (breathing in). Once there, it goes to the blood, which carries it to the rest of the body's cells. Carbon dioxide takes the reverse trip: it is produced in the cells as

Exhalation—breathing, or blowing out—is the process by which carbon dioxide leaves the body.

a waste product of metabolism, carried by the blood to the lungs, and expelled during exhalation (breathing out).

Along with the mouth, or *oral cavity,* the outermost part of the respiratory system is the nose. Its primary respiratory function is to warm, cleanse, and moisten the air. The skin deep inside the nose is a special type called *ciliated columnar epithelium,* equipped with cells called *goblet cells.* Goblet cells produce mucus, which catches dust and bacteria and prevents them from reaching the lungs. Tiny hairs called the *cilia,* located under the mucous coat, move mucus and any captured impurities to the upper airways, where they may be expelled by coughing.

The *pharynx* is the chamber behind and below the nasal cavity. The lower, frontal part of the pharynx, the *oropharynx,* contains the tongue and teeth and is actually a part of the digestive system. The upper rear part, through which air passes from the nose on its way to the lungs, is the *nasopharynx* and is part of the respiratory system.

Below the pharynx lies the larynx. Over the larynx is a flap of tissue called the *epiglottis,* which covers the larynx when swallowing occurs, preventing any food or drink from entering the airway. Inside the larynx, in the *glottis,* are the white membranes of the *vocal cords.* Inhaling automatically widens the opening between the vocal cords so that air may pass between them easily.

At the bottom of the larynx is the opening to the *trachea,* or windpipe. The trachea is a tube held in shape by about 20 horseshoe-shaped cartilage rings covered with tough elastic membrane. (Cartilage is flexible bonelike tissue.) At the back of the trachea is a layer of *smooth muscle,* the kind of muscle not subject to conscious control by the mind, that can pull the open ends of the cartilage rings together to decrease the diameter of the trachea. If foreign matter enters the trachea, these muscles constrict to prevent it from slipping deeper into the airway.

About two inches below the *suprasternal notch* (the bony notch at the base of the throat where the neck meets the chest) the trachea divides into two branches: the right and left *mainstem bronchi* (*bronchi* is the plural of the Latin word *bronchus,* meaning "branch"). Each mainstem bronchus leads to one of the lungs. In the chest, the lungs are divided by the *mediastinum,* the middle area inside the chest. The heart, esophagus, trachea, and the body's main blood vessels are in the mediastinum, under the chest's flat middle bone, the *sternum.*

On either side of the mediastinum, the lungs are covered by a tough, slippery membrane called the *pulmonary pleura.* A portion of this membrane also lines the chest cavity, where it is called the *parietal pleura.* Deep grooves in the lungs mark their division into lobes, or parts. The left lung is made up of two lobes; the right lung has three. (This is because the heart takes up more space on the left.) In the lungs, the main stem bronchi branch yet again to form the *lobar bronchi,* one leading to each lobe.

In the lobes, the bronchi divide again into *segmental bronchi:* 10 in the right lung, 9 in the left. A segmental bronchus carries air to a section of the lung called a *segment.* After the bronchi have divided into segmental bronchi, they divide as many as 20 more times, eventually forming tiny tubes only four-hundredths of an inch in diameter. These small tubes are the *terminal bronchioles.* The shape of the whole bronchial system is like the shape of a tree, with the trachea as the trunk and the terminal bronchioles as its smallest branches. In fact, the bronchial system as a whole is often called the pulmonary (breathing) tree.

Each of the terminal bronchioles—there are from 20,000 to 80,000 in each lung—ends in a berry-shaped structure called an *acinus.* In the acini lie the respiratory *bronchioles.* These smallest of all bronchioles lead to the *alveolar ducts,* and from the alveolar ducts to the very ends of the bronchi and into the *alveoli*—the lung's tiny, thin-walled air sacs (each measuring approximately 100 microns in diameter). Each lung contains from 300 to 400 million alveoli, and each alveolus is surrounded by a tiny blood vessel, called a *capillary.*

Once air reaches the alveolus, a crucial event takes place. Through the alveolar membrane, the oxygen from the air moves from the lung and into the blood. Oxygen is able to do this for two reasons. First, the membrane is permeable to oxygen (it lets oxygen pass through). Second, gases (materials that have neither independent shape nor volume) tend to move from places where there is a higher concentration of them to places where there is a lower concentration of them. So oxygen naturally moves from a place where it is plentiful (the alveolus) to a place where it is scarcer (blood). This process—moving from an area of high concentration to an area of lower concentration—is called *diffusion;* when it occurs through a membrane it is called *osmosis.*

After the oxygen enters the blood vessel, it moves by osmosis into a red blood cell. There it is held by a material called *hemoglobin.* Hemoglobin greatly increases the oxygen-carrying capacity of the blood. Without it, the heart would have to pump 130 liters of blood per minute to get enough oxygen to the cells (a liter equals about 4 cups). But blood containing hemoglobin can carry 26 times more oxygen, so the heart must only pump about 5 liters of blood per minute in the body of an adult hu-

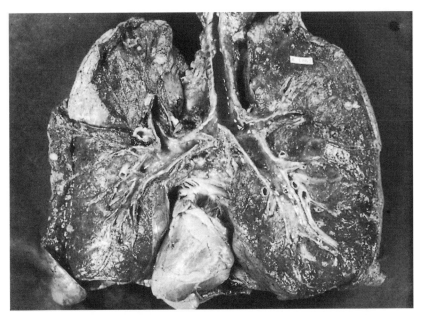

A rear view of healthy lungs and, at their base, the heart. Deep grooves in the lungs mark their division into separate lobes.

man being. Once the blood has carried the oxygen to the vicinity of a body cell, the hemoglobin lets go of the oxygen (chemical and temperature conditions cause it to do so). Next, the oxygen passes from the blood vessel into the cell where it is to be used. As before, it moves by osmosis—this time because there is less oxygen in the cell than in the blood. In the cell, the oxygen enters into the process of metabolism.

Metabolism is a very complex topic. Many chemical reactions must occur to transform the energy held in food molecules. One segment of these reactions is known as the *Krebs cycle*. The Krebs cycle is a series of chemical reactions inside a cell, in which molecules from food—proteins, fats, and sugars (derived from carbohydrates)—are broken down into smaller molecules. Each time chemical bonds of a food molecule are broken, some energy is released. First, a complex chemical reaction breaks food molecules down to produce a substance called *acetyl coenzyme A*. Next, in the first step of the Krebs cycle, acetyl coenzyme A reacts with oxaloacetic acid to produce citric acid and energy. In step two, citric acid breaks down to produce ketoglutaric acid and energy. In step three, the ketoglutaric acid breaks down to produce succinic acid and energy. In the fourth step of the Krebs cycle, succinic acid breaks down to oxaloacetic acid and energy. The oxaloacetic acid produced in the fourth step then combines with more acetyl coenzyme A, and the Krebs cycle starts over again. Two main by-products of the cell's metabolic process are water and carbon dioxide.

Carbon dioxide moves out of the body cell and into the blood (again by osmosis, because there is more carbon dioxide in the cell than in the blood). Next, it attaches to hemoglobin and travels in the blood until it reaches the lungs. There, carbon dioxide passes from the blood to the alveoli (because there is more carbon dioxide in the blood than in the alveoli). Finally, carbon dioxide is expelled from the lungs when the body exhales.

Other systems of the body also contribute to the task of breathing. The *diaphragm,* for instance, is a sheetlike muscle separating the chest from the abdomen. When the diaphragm contracts, it moves downward into the abdomen. This enlarges the chest cavity, so that air will flow in to fill the newly enlarged space. The ribs and muscles in the chest wall also contract to help enlarge the chest cavity. When they relax, the chest

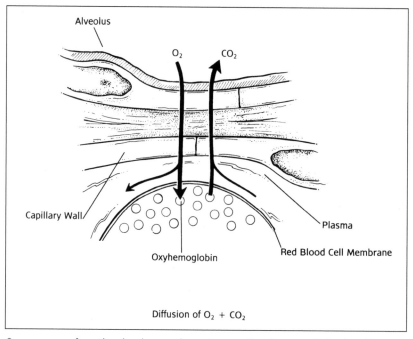

Oxygen passes from the alveolar membrane to a capillary by osmosis. During this process, molecules move from an area that contains a great deal of oxygen to an area that has little.

cavity shrinks, producing exhalation. When breathing is labored (often a symptom of respiratory illness such as pneumonia) muscles in the shoulders and neck may help the process; these are called the accessory muscles of breathing.

The nervous system helps provide the stimulus to breathe, as do organs in the blood vessels that sense when the blood needs more oxygen or is carrying too much carbon dioxide. The blood's oxygen level is sensed by groups of special cells called the *carotid body* and the *aortic body.* The carotid body is located in a large blood vessel, the *carotid artery,* in the neck. The aortic body is located inside another blood vessel, the *aorta*—the main vessel from the heart to the body. When blood near them contains too little oxygen, these two bodies send messages to the brain, which then signals the need for more rapid breathing.

Areas of the brain called the *respiratory centers* are responsible for sensing the level of carbon dioxide in the blood. There are at least four such centers: the *inspiratory center,* the *expiratory center,* the *apneustic center,* and the *pneumotaxic center.* Raising or lowering the carbon dioxide content of the blood causes the respiratory centers to stimulate either faster and deeper or slower and shallower breaths.

At the beginning of each breath, the brain sends a message down the spinal cord to the *phrenic nerve,* which is connected to the diaphragm. In response, the diaphragm contracts and moves downward. At the same time, muscles between the ribs contract, moving the ribs and the sternum outward. Consequently, the chest cavity enlarges.

Before this breath began, the chest wall was pressing on the lungs—exerting positive pressure on them. But now the chest wall, moving away from the lungs, exerts negative pressure. (Negative pressure can be seen in action by putting a straw in a glass of water and sucking on it. Water flows up, because negative pressure is being exerted on it.)

In much the same way, the outward motion of the chest wall draws the sides of the lungs outward, enlarging not only the chest cavity but the lungs, too. The result is that air flows into the newly enlarged space. As air continues flowing into the lungs, it inflates the alveoli at the end of the bronchioles. When the newly enlarged space inside the chest cavity (and inside the lungs) fills, air flow stops. The lungs are inflated and inhalation is over.

The events of inhalation are active: the body uses energy to breathe in. But to exhale the body simply relaxes. This is because the lungs and chest are springy; they simply snap back to their original shape, pushing the air out. But the lungs do not empty completely; if they did, the alveoli would collapse, increasing the work needed to inhale the next time. (Imagine blowing up a balloon; one needs to blow hard to expand it that first little bit. But after it is slightly expanded, inflating it is easier.) Finally, blood is always circulating through the lungs to pick up oxygen. If they emptied completely, some of this circulation would be useless. But, in fact, even if a person exhales as much air as possible, about one-fifth of the lungs' air capacity remains filled. This portion of air, called the *residual volume,* ensures that blood circulating through the lungs will always find oxygen and be able to give off carbon dioxide—the two main jobs of the body's respiratory system.

5

THE CIRCULATORY SYSTEM

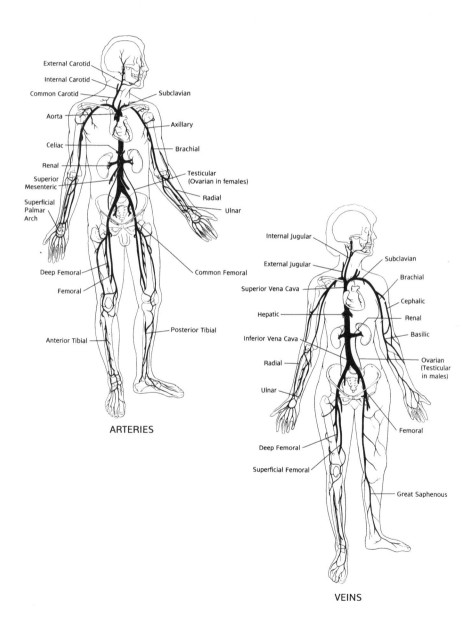

ARTERIES

External Carotid
Internal Carotid
Common Carotid
Subclavian
Aorta
Axillary
Celiac
Brachial
Renal
Testicular (Ovarian in females)
Superior Mesenteric
Radial
Superficial Palmar Arch
Ulnar
Deep Femoral
Common Femoral
Femoral
Posterior Tibial
Anterior Tibial

VEINS

Internal Jugular
External Jugular
Subclavian
Brachial
Superior Vena Cava
Cephalic
Hepatic
Renal
Inferior Vena Cava
Basilic
Radial
Ovarian (Testicular in males)
Ulnar
Femoral
Deep Femoral
Superficial Femoral
Great Saphenous

The blood-transport system that delivers oxygen and fuel to the body's cells and removes their waste products is the circulatory system. This bodily structure consists of the heart—the body's blood pump—and about 60,000 miles of blood vessels, the tubes through which blood flows. Day and night, the heart pumps at a rate of about 70 times per minute, moving the body's whole supply of blood—about 10 pints—through the system 1,000 times in each 24-hour period.

The heart itself is a muscular structure about the size of a fist. Inside, it is divided into four chambers: the two top chambers are the left and right *atria,* and the two lower chambers are the left and right *ventricles.* The atria bring blood into the heart; the ventricles pump the blood out again. At the heart's entries—one at each of the atria—valves keep blood from leaking backward out of the atria. The *tricuspid valve* lies between the right atrium and right ventricle, and the *mitral valve* prevents backup between the left ventricle and atrium. The heart's exits, one from each ventricle, also have valves to keep blood from backing up into the heart. Two additional valves, one between the right atrium and right ventricle and one between the left atrium and left ventricle, keep blood from backing up inside the heart itself. Thus blood always moves in the correct direction—into, through, and out of the heart.

To understand how the heart works, however, it is best to think of it as being divided into the right heart (right atrium and right ventricle) and the left heart (left atrium and left ventricle). This is because the heart actually does two jobs: it pumps "used" blood to the lungs, which supply oxygen and remove carbon dioxide, and it pumps "refreshed" blood, cleansed and oxygen rich, out to the body. The blood's route from the right heart to the lungs and back is the *pulmonary* circulation. The route from the left heart to the body and back is the *systemic* circulation.

To understand this, assume that the heart has just beat one time. As it did so, its left atrium contracted, squeezing oxygen-rich blood down into the left ventricle. Next, the left ventricle contracted, pumping the blood out into the aorta—the main vessel from the heart to the body. This one-two squeeze—the heart's beat—sent the blood on its way through the systemic circulation.

The aorta branches into smaller and smaller vessels called *arteries,* carrying the blood out to the head, the digestive system, and the arms and legs. Two arteries, the *coronary arteries,* double back to carry blood to the heart muscle itself. Smaller branches, the *arterioles,* divide in turn into smaller arteries called capillaries, from which blood delivers its

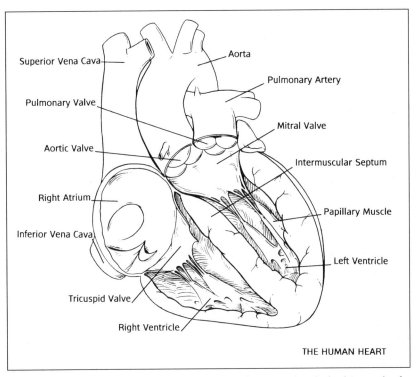

Superior Vena Cava

Aorta

Pulmonary Artery

Pulmonary Valve

Mitral Valve

Aortic Valve

Intermuscular Septum

Right Atrium

Papillary Muscle

Inferior Vena Cava

Left Ventricle

Tricuspid Valve

Right Ventricle

THE HUMAN HEART

The human heart pumps at a rate of 70 beats per minute, moving the body's supply of blood—approximately 10 pints—through the circulatory system 1,000 times during each 24-hour period.

cargo of oxygen and nutrients to the body's cells. Here also, blood picks up the cells' waste products.

The capillaries merge with *venules*, the smallest veins that carry blood back toward the heart. The venules merge with bigger and bigger veins, finally joining the *venae cavae*, the largest of the body's back-toward-the-heart vessels. The venae cavae empty the blood into the heart's right atrium—and the blood's journey through the systemic circulation is complete.

The blood must also pick up new oxygen supplies and get rid of the waste products it collected from the cells. To do this, it must travel to the lungs, through the pulmonary circulation. From the right atrium, blood travels down to the right ventricle and out through the *pulmonary artery*—the main blood vessel that leads to the lungs. In the lungs, blood moves through smaller and smaller veins until it reaches the capillaries, the tiny vessels around the alveoli. There the blood picks up oxygen and drops off the carbon dioxide it got from the body's cells.

Next, the lungs' capillaries merge with tiny vessels leading back toward the heart, eventually reaching the pulmonary veins—the lungs' main vessels leading to the heart. The pulmonary veins empty the blood into the left atrium, completing the blood's pulmonary-circulation journey.

In this way, blood travels endlessly through the body—from the left heart to the body's cells, from the body back to the right heart, from the right heart to the lungs, and finally from the lungs back to the left heart, for the beginning of another round trip.

Although they may seem like separate processes, the pulmonary and systemic circulations do not take place at different times and are not entirely distinct from one another. Instead, they are occurring simultaneously. To power them the heart's right and left sides work together. The two top chambers receive blood at the same time—the left side from the lungs, the right side from the body. Then both atria squeeze at the same time, sending their loads of blood down to the two ventricles. About three-fifths of a second later, the ventricles pump simultaneously. The classic "lub-dub" of a heartbeat is the sound of this cooperation: the "lub" is the sound of the two atria pushing blood down into the ventricles at the same moment. The "dub" is the sound the two ventricles make as each one pushes its load of blood: the left ventricle pumping toward the body while the right pumps toward the lungs.

The "bump" of the pulse, which can be felt on the side of the neck or in the wrist, is caused by a slight expansion of the artery each time the heart pumps. The blood pressure is a measurement of how much force the blood is exerting against the walls of the vessels and other body structures. The force varies according to how forcefully the heart pumps, how much blood it pumps per beat, and how easily the vessels let blood pass through them. Usually two different pressures are measured: the *systolic* pressure when the ventricles are pumping and the *diastolic* pressure between heartbeats as the heart relaxes. When a doctor or nurse measures one's blood pressure, the higher number, or the one "on top," is the systolic pressure; the lower one, or the "bottom" number, is the diastolic.

The rate of the heart's beat is set by a small knot of nervelike tissue in the right atrium. This knot, called the *sinoatrial node*, fires off a tiny nerve impulse that causes both atria to contract. (This is also known as the electrical conduction system of the heart.) The impulse is also sent

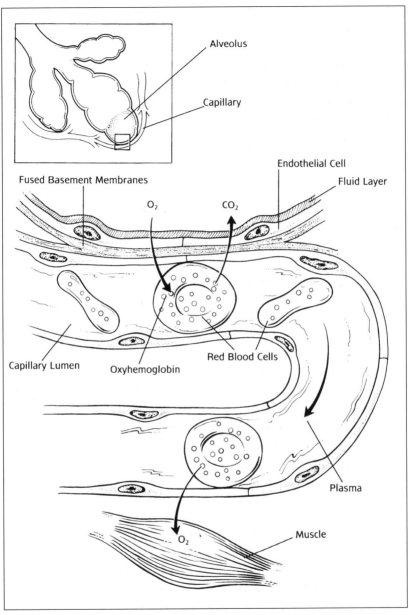

Oxygen diffuses from the alveolar membrane into a capillary, where it is picked up by a hemoglobin molecule, transported to a group of cells, and then released.

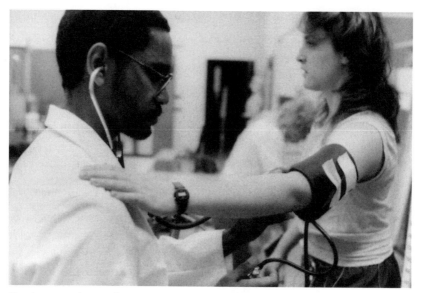

Blood pressure is actually a measurement of how much force the blood is exerting against the walls of the vessels and other body structures.

to a similar node in the right ventricle, called the *ventricular node.* From there the impulse travels along nerve fibers to the ventricles, causing them to contract in unison just after the atria have contracted.

The heart rate and the force of each heartbeat are also affected by two major nerve pathways from the brain: the vagus nerve, whose action tends to slow the heart and lessen the force of a beat, and a chain of nerve fibers from the sympathetic nervous system, whose action tends to speed up heart rate and increase the force of a beat. Both kinds of nerves originate in the part of the brain called the medulla, which contains a cardiac inhibitory (slowing) center that sends nerve impulses to the heart via the vagus nerve and a cardiac accelerator (speeding) center that sends impulses along the middle, superior, and inferior cardiac nerves. Impulses travel from the medulla down the spinal cord and reach the heart at areas called cardiac plexuses, located near the aorta. Most of the vagus and accelerator fibers entering the heart at the cardiac plexuses end at the heart's sinoatrial node—the heart's "pacemaker"—but a few terminate in the ventricular node or in the heart muscle itself.

When the vagus nerve is sending more impulses than is the accelerator nerve (during periods of rest or sleep, for instance), its influence—slowing—is greater, and the heart rate tends to slow down. This is because the vague-nerve signals cause the release of a chemical called acetylcholine in the sinoatrial node, and acetylcholine slows the node's firing rate.

But when the accelerator nerves are sending more impulses, their influence—speeding up the heart—is greater and the heart rate rises. This is because the accelerator nerves cause the release of a chemical called epinephrine, which makes the node fire faster and the muscle contract more forcefully.

Fear, for instance, speeds the heart rate when the brain's medulla gets nerve signals from the thinking area of the brain (the cerebral cortex) and brain structures that produce emotions (the limbic system). In response, the medulla sends "speed up" signals along the accelerator nerves to the heart, so the heart will pump blood faster and harder; thus the whole body will have a plentiful blood supply so it can be ready to fight, run away, or do whatever the dangerous situation requires.

The blood vessels in the body are of two main types: arteries, which carry blood from the left heart to the body, and veins, which return blood from the body to the heart. Both arteries and veins are tubes made of three layers: the inner layer is made of epithelial (skinlike) tissue; the middle layer is muscular; and the outer layer is formed of connective tissue, fibrous cells that hold the vessel together. Because blood in the arteries is under more pressure than blood in the veins, the artery walls are thicker and have more muscle tissue than do those of the veins. Some veins have tiny valvelike flaps of tissue within them, to keep blood moving in the right direction: to the heart.

The blood, carrier of nutrients, oxygen, and wastes for the entire body, has two main components: *corpuscles,* two kinds of cells that do different jobs, and *plasma,* clear fluid in which the cells are suspended. In the plasma are three main proteins: *albumin, globulin,* and *fibrinogen.* Albumin and globulin help plasma maintain the proper thickness and chemical balance; fibrinogen helps the blood to clot.

Albumin, a substance made in the liver, consists of very tiny protein molecules floating in the blood plasma—the liquid part of blood. Molecules of albumin tend to attract plasma and to hold it within the blood vessels. Thus by retaining plasma that would otherwise tend to leak more copiously through vessel walls, albumin helps maintain the fluid balance of the circulatory system.

Globulins are proteins that have three main functions: alpha and beta globulins help transport substances in the blood, such as food molecules, by combining with the molecules. Gamma globulins help fight off invaders by transporting the antibodies produced by the immune system to sites where they are needed.

Fibrinogen is the protein that makes blood clot; thus it prevents excess bleeding from injuries. Enzymes released from damaged vessels cause fibrinogen to change into tiny strands of a substance called fibrin, which forms a network and solidifies into the blood clot itself.

The red blood cells are the most numerous of all cells in blood: 5.5 million per cubic millimeter. The main job of the red cell is to carry oxygen via hemoglobin, a material that turns bright red when oxygen attaches to it. This is why arterial blood—blood carrying lots of oxygen—is bright red. Red blood cells are constantly being produced in bone marrow, the soft tissue inside some bones, to replace red cells that die normally after about 120 days.

Platelets make up another part of the blood, and close to 300,000 can be found in a cubic inch of human blood. Indeed, there are more platelets in the blood than white blood cells, although there are fewer platelets than red blood cells.

Another kind of cell in blood is the white cell: blood contains 4,000 to 10,000 of these per cubic centimeter. Their main job is defense: to attack, engulf, and digest invaders such as disease-causing bacteria.

Among the invaders the white blood cells will battle are foreign blood cells; this is why blood transfusions were dangerous before scientists divided blood into types that could safely be taken from one person and given to another (these are types O, A, B, and AB). Another way of grouping blood types is by rhesus factor, or Rh factor, another inherited blood characteristic. If an infant's parents differ in their Rh factors, the infant can have potentially fatal blood problems, but blood transfusions can usually reverse them.

Sometimes such problems occur before an infant's birth, but this can now be detected if the woman seeks prenatal care. Before birth, all an infant's needs are supplied by its mother. Because the unborn infant gets its oxygen and nutrients from its mother's blood, the infant needs some way of transferring these substances out of its mother's blood and into its own. The process is accomplished in this manner: two umbilical arteries and an umbilical vein make up the umbilical cord—the tissue that connects the unborn infant with a structure called the placenta. The placenta is a tissue connecting the umbilical cord with the wall of the uterus, the organ containing the unborn infant. To obtain oxygen and nutrients from the mother's

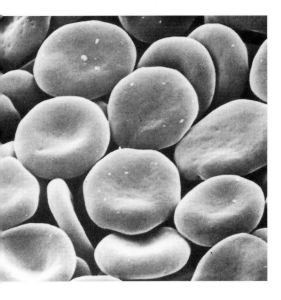

An electron micrograph of red blood cells magnified 5,000 times. The primary function of red blood cells is to carry oxygen to the cells via hemoglobin.

blood in the placenta, the infant's blood comes from two vessels in its lower abdomen, the *internal iliac arteries,* to the umbilical cord where it flows through the umbilical arteries to the placenta. In the placenta the infant's blood moves through tiny capillaries that lie very near capillaries filled with the mother's blood. Oxygen and nutrients diffuse from the mother's capillaries into the infant's capillaries. The oxygen- and nutrient-enriched blood returns to the infant's body through the umbilical vein.

In the infant's body, a small amount of the enriched blood goes to the liver. The rest travels through a continuation of the umbilical vein called the *ductus venosus* into a main vessel called the *inferior vena cava,* which empties into the right atrium of the heart. Because it already carries oxygen from the mother's blood, however, it does not need to travel to the infant's lungs (which do not contain air anyway). So from the right atrium blood moves instead through a hole called the *foramen ovale* into the left atrium of the heart. From the left atrium, the infant's blood travels down the pulmonary artery and through yet another opening, the *ductus arteriosus,* into the *descending thoracic aorta.* The aorta carries the oxygen- and nutrient-rich blood out of the infant's body.

When the infant is born, however, it begins taking in oxygen through its own lungs. Therefore its blood must travel through the lungs to pick up oxygen instead of receiving it through the placenta. So at birth the infant's circulation must change in this way: almost immediately after the infant takes its first breath, the foremen ovale and ductus arteriosus close. This blocks off the "bypass route" that sent blood from the right atrium to the left atrium and then directly out to the infant's body. From now on the blood is pumped from the right atrium to the right ventricle, and then from the right ventricle to the lungs, from the lungs to the left atrium, from the left atrium to the left ventricle, and finally to the infant's body.

6

THE DIGESTIVE SYSTEM

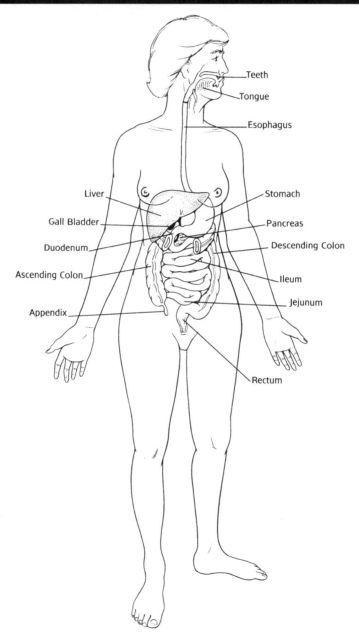

Teeth

Tongue

Esophagus

Liver

Stomach

Gall Bladder

Pancreas

Duodenum

Descending Colon

Ascending Colon

Ileum

Jejunum

Appendix

Rectum

The foods people eat are loaded with nutrients the body needs for fuel and for its very survival. These nutrients include carbohydrates, proteins, fats, minerals, vitamins, and water. Water, which is not often mentioned as a nutrient in itself, is very important to the body's proper functioning. It lubricates the body's organs, regulates blood pressure, and prevents dehydration. In fact, the human body can live longer without food than without water. All of the nutrients help the body regulate itself and provide for proper body maintenance and repair. Carbohydrates, fats, and proteins serve as fuel for the body—giving a person energy to perform daily tasks.

Carbohydrates are found in two types—sugars and starches—and are chemically composed of carbon, hydrogen, and oxygen. Carbohydrates are easily processed and used by the body to produce energy, but they are not as rich in energy as are fats. Some starch carbohydrates include breads, rice, pasta, and potatoes. Sugar carbohydrates are found in milk, nuts, fruits, and, of course, in many desserts.

Fats are found in dairy products, meats, nuts, oils, and egg yolks. Although the body does need a small amount of fat to function properly, an excess can lead to some serious troubles, such as heart disease. Every cell in the body needs proteins for both growth and repair. These proteins, which make up close to 18% of the human body's weight, can be found in such foods as meat, fish, milk, eggs, beans, and whole grains.

Naturally, the complex chemical structures of all these nutrients must be broken down before the body's cells can use them. This takes place through a process called digestion. The first step in this procedure is chewing, as the teeth break food pieces into smaller bits. Chewing also mixes food with saliva (fluid from glands under the tongue, called salivary glands). Although it is watery, saliva is more than a moistening agent, for it contains digestive enzymes: chemicals that break complex molecules into smaller, simpler molecules.

The main enzyme in saliva is *ptyalin,* which begins breaking down carbohydrate molecules into the sugar maltose. While ptyalin is still working on the carbohydrates, the food is swallowed. It moves down the throat to the esophagus, the muscles of which contract and relax in a rippling motion called *peristalsis.* This action moves the food on and into the stomach, a hollow, muscular reservoir that holds food for further processing.

Digestion requires the help of several different substances. One of these is *gastrin,* an enzyme produced by the lower part of the stomach and released into the bloodstream, where it is carried to the whole

The body must receive the recommended amounts of proteins, carbohydrates, fats, vitamins, and minerals—all found in food—to maintain itself properly.

stomach. Gastrin causes stomach cells to release two more substances, hydrochloric acid and *pepsin,* which begin breaking protein in foods into simpler molecules called *peptones.* The mucous lining of the stomach keeps the acid from harming the rest of the stomach wall. Food may remain in the stomach for as long as 4 hours (and in the entire digestive system for anywhere from 2 to 15 hours) while it is gradually being broken down to a thick, acidic liquid called *chyme.*

From the base of the stomach, peristalsis moves chyme through the *pyloric valve* (a muscular area at the lower end of the stomach that can squeeze shut to keep the contents of the stomach from flowing back into the stomach) into the *duodenum.* The duodenum comprises the first 10 or 12 inches of the small intestine (which is 18 to 21 feet long and has a diameter of 1 ½ inches) and is curved in the shape of the letter C. Here, food is broken down even further by four more chemicals: *bile,* which is made by the liver and stored in the gall bladder, and *trypsin, lipase,* and *amylase,* all of which are enzymes produced by the pancreas.

The primary function of bile is to break down fats, working on them until they are just tiny drops. When this is accomplished, lipase breaks the fats down into two simpler substances: glycerol and fatty acid. At the same time, trypsin works on the peptones (protein broken down in the stomach), breaking them into even simpler chemicals called *peptides*. And amylase works on remaining carbohydrates, breaking them down into maltose.

After being broken down, the food travels farther down the small intestine to the *jejunum* (the 8 or 9 feet of intestine following the duodenum) and the *ileum* (the end section, 8 to 11 feet in length). Much like the stomach, the small intestine has glands that produce a thick mucous lining that prevents the intestine from digesting itself with intestinal juices. Here, in the intestine, the simple chemicals that were once the food begin to be absorbed through the intestine's walls, through millions of tiny protrusions called *villi*. Each villus contains a tiny blood vessel and a tiny *lacteal*—a branch of the lymph system, a network of fluid-filled channels throughout the body. The blood vessels in the villi absorb maltose from the carbohydrate breakdown. Enzymes in the villi break the maltose down even further, into glucose, fructose, or galactose—three simple sugar molecules. If the villi do not contain the right enzymes, certain kinds of sugars will not be broken down correctly. Some people, for example, do not have the enzyme lactase in the villi of their small intestine. Lactase is the enzyme that breaks down lactose—a kind of sugar that comes from milk. This enzyme shortage, often an inherited problem, is called *lactase deficiency*. It is the reason why some people cannot drink milk or eat milk products such as cheese. They do not have the right enzyme to digest these foods.

Once they reach the villi, the simple chemicals are absorbed and sent to where they are needed. Amino acids and simple sugars move into the blood capillaries and finally into the bloodstream. Fats pass into the lacteals, into the lymph system, and out through large lymph ducts into the bloodstream. From the bloodstream, the simple sugars travel in the blood to the liver, where they are stored as *glycogen,* the fuel used by the body cells to make energy. Glycogen storage in the liver helps ensure that the body always has a backup supply of fuel.

The peptides travel through the bloodstream to the liver and there receive a final breakdown in a process called *deamination.* The simple molecules thus produced from proteins are called amino acids. The liver sends the amino acids back into the blood for transport to the cells, which use them to make dozens of protein-based substances: elements of blood that help it thicken and clot, enzymes that facilitate chemical reactions all over the body, and building blocks to make the tissues for the body's growth, development, and healing.

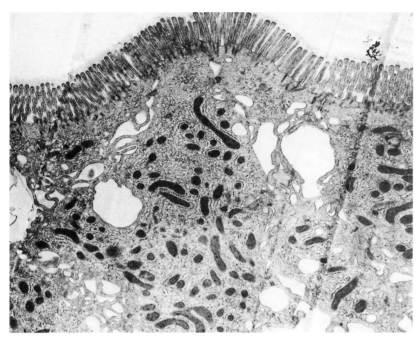

An electron micrograph of the villi in the small intestine enlarged 6,000 times. Digested nutrients pass through the pores of the villi and into the blood vessels inside.

The blood vessels carry the fatty acids to the body's cells, where the fats are split by enzymes into *cholesterol, phospholipids,* and *triglycerides.* Cholesterol is sent back through the bloodstream to the liver, which in turn shunts it back to the lower intestine to be removed from the body. Not all cholesterol, however, leaves the body. As most people now know, this steroid alcohol can build up in the bloodstream and lead to very serious medical problems. Cholesterol moves about in the bloodstream wrapped in water-soluble proteins known as lipoproteins. These lipoproteins can be either low density or high density. High-density lipoproteins return to the liver for digestion. Low-density lipoproteins, however, travel through the blood and may end up clogging arteries.

The human body produces all the cholesterol it will ever need. Unfortunately, many people consume an excess of fatty meats and other foods containing saturated fats. Doctors are able to measure blood cholesterol and can recommend diets and medication if cholesterol levels are high. Unfortunately, more than half of all American adults have cholesterol counts that exceed the suggested guidelines. This may make

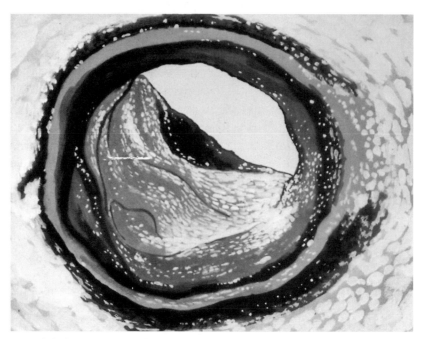

An occluded artery. The round, ringed shape is the artery itself, and the materials inside of it are fatty deposits. Buildup of fats in the arteries can cause heart disease.

them especially susceptible to *atherosclerosis,* a disease that involves the deterioration of the arterial linings.

Another type of fat, triglycerides, may be sent to the fat-storage areas of the body—layers of fat that collect under the skin—or may enter muscle cells and be used to supply energy needed by the cells. Phospholipids, essential for the production of cell walls in the body's growth, development, and healing, go to the liver, where they are stored for later use.

Vitamins and minerals—tiny quantities of substances the body cells need—are originally contained in foods and reach the cells by two routes: Some vitamins, such as vitamins B and C, are dissolved in water and absorbed along with it through the small intestine. Any excess of them, still dissolved in water, is removed from the body by the kidney. This means the body cannot build up excess amounts of water-soluble vitamins, but it also means the body stores no reserve supply of them. Thus water-soluble vitamins must be steadily supplied in food.

Vitamins that dissolve only in fat, such as vitamins D, K, A, and E, can only travel in fat molecules. This means excess supplies cannot be excreted by the kidneys (because the kidneys can only excrete chemicals dissolved in water). Instead, fat-soluble vitamins are stored in the liver. So the body usually has a reserve supply of fat-soluble vitamins, but the liver can build up amounts that are large enough to be harmful. Minerals such as calcium and iron (absorbed mostly in the small intestine in a number of different, complex ways), are also stored by the body. Thus reserve supplies of many minerals are available in the body's stores, but some of these too may build up in harmful amounts.

Once the useful products of food digestion have been absorbed through the villi of the small intestine, the leftover matter—indigestible material—moves into the large intestine. It is important that this indigestible matter contain some fiber, also called roughage, so the walls of the large intestine will be able to move the waste matter efficiently. Fiber can be found in the cell walls of plants such as celery and lettuce and in the grains of cereal grasses such as oats and wheat. The rough edges of these substances help stimulate the colon's muscles so the waste matter is sent on to the rectum and expelled (as material called feces) from the body.

Meanwhile, the very simple molecules that emerge as a result of digestion are absorbed by the body's cells. The proteins are used as building blocks, and carbohydrates and fats are used for energy. The many varieties and methods of reassembling simple proteins into the body's cells, tissues, and organs are much too varied and complex to detail here. They include making new blood cells, repairing injured skin, adding cells for growth and development, and all the other building functions of the body.

The other purpose of food—making energy—also occurs by a varied and complex series of steps. The early parts of a cell's energy-making activities vary greatly depending upon the type of cell and on whether the energy is being derived from fats or from carbohydrates. Simplified, the final steps in the process are always as follows:

1. Complex reactions inside the cell turn simple food-derived molecules into molecules of adenosine triphosphate, or ATP.

2. An enzyme called hexokinase breaks ATP into two simpler molecules: adenosine diphosphate, or ADP, and glucose-6-phosphate.

3. Glucose-6-phosphate is broken down by the enzyme phosphates into a chemical called pyruvate.

4. Pyruvate enters into chemical reaction with oxygen.

In this reaction, the bonds holding the pyruvate molecule together are broken, and their energy is released. The by-products of the reaction, carbon dioxide and water, are removed; the energy remains for the cell to use.

In short, the process of digestion breaks food into simple substances, which the body uses as raw materials—building blocks—and as a source of fuel to power all the processes of life.

7

THE URINARY SYSTEM

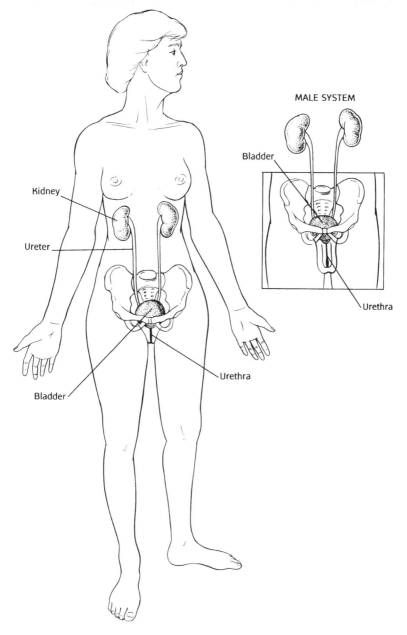

MALE SYSTEM

Bladder

Kidney

Ureter

Urethra

Urethra

Bladder

Metabolism—the sum of the energy-producing processes that go on inside the body's cells—creates waste products, much as a fire creates ashes. And just as a fire may be smothered by too many ashes, the body can be injured if waste products build up in it. The respiratory system removes a large portion of one main waste, carbon dioxide. The major portion of the body's other wastes—mostly toxic chemicals and excess water, along with some carbon dioxide dissolved in water—are removed by the kidneys, which are the major organs of the urinary system.

But waste removal is not the only chore of this system: the kidneys also perform four other very important jobs in the body. They keep the body's fluid level balanced so it is neither too wet nor too dry for proper functioning. They help maintain healthy bones by keeping the right level of calcium (an important bone-building mineral) in the blood. They stimulate the body to make red blood cells to replace cells that wear out. And they help regulate blood pressure—how hard the blood pushes against the body's arteries, veins, and organs as it is pumped through them. All these functions are smaller chores related to the kidney's main task: filtering waste from the blood, dissolving the waste in water, and sending this water, called urine, out of the body.

Each of the body's two kidneys is a reddish, bean-shaped organ; they are located on each side of the spine at about waist level, with the upper part of the kidney extending up under the lower ribs. On the inner edge of each kidney is an opening called the *hilus;* through it pass the organ's arteries and veins, its nerves, and a funnel-shaped structure called the *renal pelvis*—the kidney's outflow tract. From the kidney, urine flows out the renal pelvis through a long tube called the *ureter,* collects in the *bladder,* and finally flows through a shorter tube, the *urethra,* which discharges the urine from the body.

The inside of the kidney consists of two main areas, a dark red outer border called the *cortex* and a lighter-colored inner area, the medulla. The *medulla is* divided into cone-shaped structures called the *renal pyramids,* whose pointed tips aim toward the renal pelvis. The tissue of the cortex covers the flat bases at the outward ends of the medulla's cones and extends down between them.

The kidney begins filtering blood and producing urine when blood flows into it through the renal artery. In the kidney's cortex, the artery branches into smaller and smaller arteries. The tiniest branches of these lead to the kidney's most basic working parts: the *nephrons.*

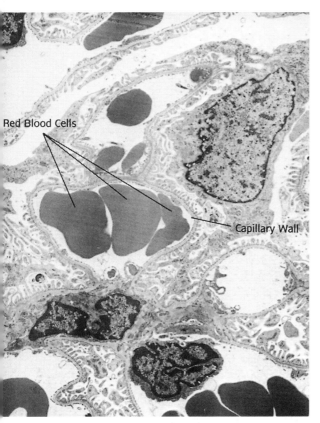

Red Blood Cells

Capillary Wall

An electron micrograph of red blood cells in the capillary wall of one of the kidney's glomeruli. Although each glomerulus is extremely tiny, the total capacity of all of the glomeruli is large enough to hold nearly one-fourth of the body's blood supply at one time.

Each of a kidney's approximately 1 million nephrons is a structure about 1⅕ inches long, with walls made of extremely thin skin cells. The root of the nephron, called the *Bowman's capsule,* lies in the cortex part of the kidney, surrounding a tuft of 30 to 40 tiny blood vessels looped together in a knotlike bunch called the *glomerulus.*

The walls of the vessels in the glomerulus are extremely thin—so thin that chemicals from the blood can pass through the vessel walls and out into the capsule itself. But even though each glomerulus is small, the total capacity of all the glomeruli is so great that about one-fourth of the body's blood supply may be in them at any one time. This is because there are so many tiny blood vessels packed into the glomeruli. As a result all the body's blood passes through the kidneys every five or six minutes.

As it does so, about one-fifth of the water in the blood passes through the vessel walls into the capsules at the nephrons' roots. Dissolved in the water are an array of chemicals: urea and ammonia, by-products of protein digestion; carbonic acid, a byproduct of energy production in the cells; creatinine, a waste product of muscle cells; and many other substances the body cannot use and must excrete. But proteins, fats, and blood cells do not pass through the vessel walls; they are too big; thus the body saves these useful materials instead of sending them to the nephron capsules.

Once waste materials pass from the blood vessels of the glomerulus into the Bowman's capsule in the cortex, they move on into a tiny tube called a *tubule*. Next—still dissolved in the water that came with them from the blood—they flow into a vast branching network of larger and larger tubules leading into the medulla. Up to 180 quarts of liquid go into the network of tubules each day.

Next, as it passes through the tubules, most of the fluid and many of the substances in it are reabsorbed back through the tubule walls, into tiny blood vessels around the tubules, and eventually back into the circulation of the blood. This happens because the body, in order to get rid of waste efficiently, initially had to send a lot of water and other materials to the glomeruli. Now, in the tubules, it reclaims much of what it sent.

The substances reclaimed by the body include all the sugars in the urine, unless the amount of sugar in the blood is too high—for very high blood sugar levels will keep some sugars from being reclaimed in the kidneys. Instead, this excess sugar will be given off as waste. Sufferers of diabetes mellitus, a disease that occurs when the pancreas fails to produce a sufficient amount of *insulin* (a hormone that checks and regulates the amount of sugar in the blood) have an excess of sugar in the urine.

The body also reclaims as much salt as it can because salt is needed for proper cell working all over the body. But the kidneys always let some salt pass into the urine, which is why people need to consume salt in moderation (most of which can be found naturally in foods and does not need to be added) every day.

In addition to keeping cells working well, the blood's salt level also helps regulate blood pressure. The kidneys manage this relationship by retaining or giving off water. If there is a lot of salt in the body, the kidneys retain water to keep the salt diluted; the increased level of body fluid raises the blood pressure. If the salt level is low, the body does not need so much water to dilute salt; so the kidneys give off more water and the blood pressure drops. This is why people with high blood pressure are advised to consume less salt: lower salt levels allow the kidneys

The kidneys control and filter bodily fluids by dissolving waste in water and then sending this liquid, called urine, out of the body.

to give off more water, and the blood pressure drops as a result. Helping the kidneys conserve or excrete water is a hormone called *aldosterone,* which is made by the adrenal glands (small glands located just above the kidneys).

The kidneys also manage the body's general acid level by retaining or giving off particles called hydrogen ions. A high percentage of hydrogen ions in the blood and body fluids makes the body acidic; a low level makes it alkaline. Acid levels may rise or fall as a result of muscle activity, high or low levels of oxygen in cells, breathing (which affects how fast the lungs give off carbon dioxide and thus changes the carbonic acid level in blood), or for a number of other reasons. High levels of acid make the renal tubules reclaim fewer hydrogen ions; low levels cause more ions to be reclaimed.

Finally, if the body has much more water than it needs, it will not reclaim some water from the tubules and instead will send it out with the waste. This keeps the heart from having to pump the extra fluid. If a water shortage in the body exists, the tubules will reclaim as much water as they can—while still excreting enough water to dissolve and carry away the waste matter. The kidney saves or gives off water in response to a hormone called *antidiuretic hormone*, which is made by the pituitary gland in the brain.

So the kidneys are always managing a lot of substances at once: getting rid of wastes but reclaiming useful substances; giving off enough

An X ray of an empty bladder (top) and a full bladder (bottom). All urine passes from the ureters into the bladder and then leaves the body through the urethra.

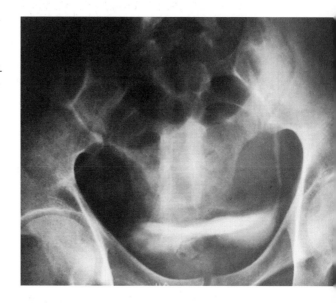

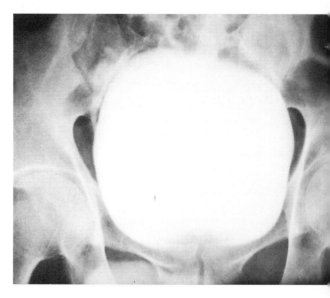

water to wash out wastes but keeping enough to maintain the body's normal water content; keeping the water/salt level balanced so blood pressure is neither too high (too much water or too much salt) nor too low (not enough water or not enough salt). And at the same time they keep acid levels normal by saving or getting rid of hydrogen ions. To help them perform this multifunction balancing act, the kidneys secrete substances that affect their own and other organs' functions. When blood pressure is too low, for instance, the kidneys send a chemical called *renin* into the blood. Renin in turn stimulates the production of *angiotensin,* an enzyme that constricts blood vessels, raising blood pressure.

Another substance produced by the kidneys is the active form of vitamin D. The kidneys take vitamin D that comes from food and—in response to low blood levels of calcium—transform the vitamin into a substance that helps the body absorb more calcium. The calcium itself is used in making and repairing bones and teeth. The kidneys also dispose of the chemical phosphorus, whose presence in blood can weaken the bones and teeth by drawing calcium from them. And the kidneys reclaim calcium from the renal tubules in response to *parahormone.* This hormone is made by the *parathyroid glands,* small glands behind the thyroid gland, which is located in the throat.

Yet another substance released by the kidneys is a protein called *erythropoietin.* It stimulates the bone marrow, the soft tissue inside bones, to make red blood cells to replace those that wear out or are damaged by disease.

When the kidneys work properly in concert with the rest of the body, the renal tubules reclaim about 99% of the water and chemicals that go through them. The rest—waste chemicals, enough water to dissolve the waste, and any extra water to be given off—flows down the tubules to the tips of the cones in the medulla. Next, this fluid—the urine—leaves the tips of the renal cones through openings called *papillae.*

Now the urine needs only to be discharged: thus it flows from the papillae down the ureters to the bladder, and from there it passes through the urethra (most adults can control this part of the process), and out of the body during a process known as urination. The amount of urine given off per day is about ¾ to 4⅕ pints, depending on body size and the amount of fluid taken in through food and drink.

The kidneys, then, are complex organs whose job is to filter the blood of waste and wash the waste from the body. In doing so they regulate salt, water, and other substances in a complicated balancing act—one that maintains the body's proper fluid and chemical equilibrium.

8

THE ENDOCRINE SYSTEM

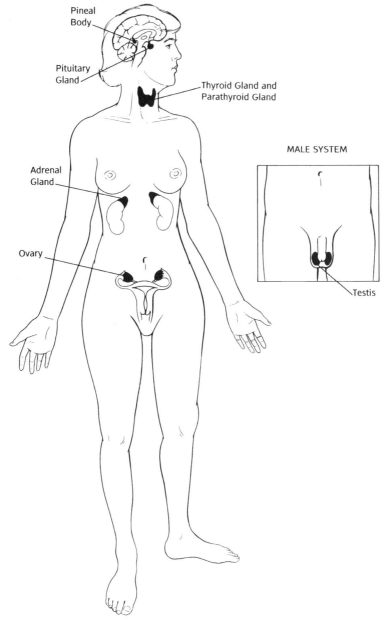

Pineal Body

Pituitary Gland

Thyroid Gland and Parathyroid Gland

MALE SYSTEM

Adrenal Gland

Ovary

Testis

The organs and systems of the body do not function in isolation. Instead, they communicate and cooperate with one another so that the body can function in an organized, efficient manner. One way the body maintains its communications is through the nervous system—the network made up of the nerves, spinal cord, and brain. The nervous system also links the body with the outside world. But the body has another "communications network" by which it keeps many of its internal parts cooperating with one another—the endocrine system.

Unlike the nervous system, however, which throughout the body is made of one kind of tissue (nerve tissue) and performs one function (transmitting nerve impulses), the endocrine system consists of many kinds of tissues, producing different substances that affect the body in a number of different ways. The parts of the endocrine system are not even directly connected to one another, unlike parts of other body systems. Rather, the one factor all of the parts of the endocrine system have in common is their purpose: the production of hormones.

Hormones help regulate and fine-tune some of the body's most important functions. They are chemical-messenger substances that—in very tiny amounts—help control functions of the body's organs and tissues. The organ that a specific hormone helps control is called its target organ. Whereas many of the body's glands send their products (sweat, saliva, mucus, and other substances including some hormones) to target organs via ducts called exocrine glands, the endocrine system sends its substances into the bloodstream. An endocrine hormone affects only its target organ, because only the target's cells are designed to receive the hormone's chemical message.

Endocrine hormones affect their target organs in three main ways:

1. Temporarily, in emergencies. The hormone adrenaline, for instance, is released in response to sudden danger. It provokes action that increases blood sugar for fast energy, heightens nerve responses for good reflexes, increases the blood supply to the brain so it is suitably alert, and brings about a wide range of other reactions that help the body handle threatening situations quickly.

2. Long term, to assist in activities the body needs to perform all the time. For instance, hormones from the thyroid gland are constantly helping to stimulate metabolism—the range of activities by which the body produces and uses energy for all its functions.

3. Short term *and* long term, to assist in functions carried on in varying degrees. For instance, hormones from glands in the reproductive system are always being produced to develop and maintain specifically male or female organs and characteristics. But during the period called puberty, which occurs between late childhood and early adulthood, the production of these hormones increases to spur development of the reproductive organs. Thus the male body prepares itself for fatherhood, and the female body prepares itself for motherhood. Changes also occur during middle age. When male or female characteristics are long established and the time for parenthood is ending, reproductive glands may lower, but not entirely cease, their production of reproductive hormones. In men, lowered reproductive hormone levels result in the production of fewer sperm cells. In females, the lowered hormone levels cause the body to cease ovulating (the cyclic release of an ovum from the *ovaries*). As a result, the reproductive system no longer goes through the monthly cycle commonly known as the menstrual cycle.

The individual glands and tissues of the endocrine system are the pituitary, thyroid, parathyroid, adrenal, pancreatic, thymus, and reproductive glands. Each gland is located, however, at a different spot in the body and is not necessarily next to the organs it affects.

The *pituitary gland is* extremely important to growth, development, and general health. It produces a number of substances vital to the proper functioning of other glands. About the size of a pea, it lies under the lower rear part of the brain in a small, bony pocket of the skull. It has two lobes, or sections: the anterior (front) lobe and the posterior (back) lobe.

The anterior lobe of the pituitary produces six hormones. Growth hormone regulates the way the body uses protein to increase body size, especially in infants, children, and young adults. Adrenocorticotropic hormone (ACTH) acts to stimulate another gland, the adrenal gland. Thyrotropic hormone is another hormone that assists a gland; it keeps the thyroid gland healthy and stimulates thyroid function. Gonadotropic hormones (follicle-stimulating hormones and luteinizing hormones) regulate functions of the male and female reproductive organs. Prolactin stimulates the mammary glands in a pregnant woman's breasts to develop and, after the infant's birth, to produce milk in order to nourish the child.

The pituitary gland produces growth hormone, a chemical substance essential to growth in infants and children.

The posterior lobe of the pituitary gland produces two hormones: antidiuretic hormone and oxytocin. Antidiuretic hormone (ADH) causes the kidneys to conserve water when the body does not have enough. When the body has more than enough water, the posterior pituitary lowers its ADH output so the kidney can give off excess water. ADH also causes smooth muscles in the arteries to contract, thus increasing blood pressure. Oxytocin causes muscles in the uterus (the chamber in a woman's body that holds the developing fetus) to contract during birth—the time when the infant emerges into the outer world. It also helps muscles in the mother's breasts contract, facilitating the flow of milk into the newborn's mouth.

The *thyroid gland* lies in the front of the neck. It has two lobes, one on either side of the trachea; the lobes are connected by a bridge of tissue known as the isthmus. The thyroid produces hormones that are released when the gland is stimulated by thyrotropic hormone from the pituitary gland. Thyroxine stimulates the body's metabolic functions. Calcitonin is a hormone that helps send calcium to bones where it is needed for growth, development, and maintenance of strong bone tissue.

The *parathyroid glands,* four small glands each about the size of a pea, lie against the surface of the thyroid gland in the neck. They produce the hormone parahormone, which helps the body take in and use calcium and phosphate salts. Parahormone also acts with calcitonin (which is also responsible for stimulating the production of parahormone) to regulate the amount of calcium in the blood.

The *adrenal glands* are a pair of wedge-shaped organs, one on top of each kidney. They have an inner part called the medulla and an outer part called the cortex. The hormones that the adrenal medulla produces are adrenaline (epinephrine), which serves to increase heart rate, raises blood sugar, and increases awareness when the body faces any sudden emergency situations, and noradrenaline (norepinephrine), which increases the blood pressure.

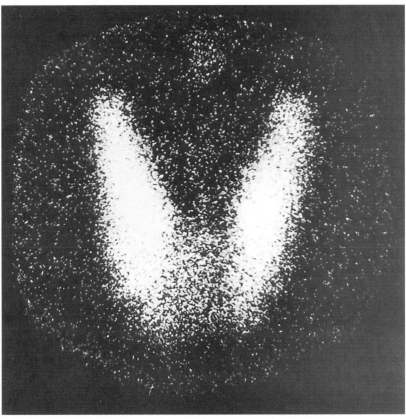

A magnified gamma scan of a human thyroid (frontal view). The thyroid gland produces thyroxine, a hormone responsible for the body's metabolic functions.

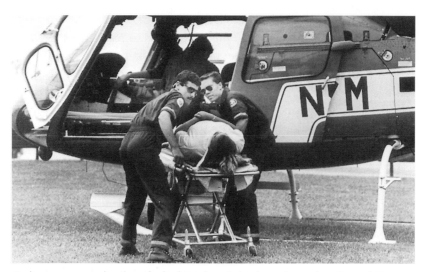

During emergency situations the body's adrenal glands produce adrenaline, which increases the heart rate, raises blood sugar, and heightens the body's awareness, and noradrenaline, which elevates blood pressure.

The hormones the cortex produces are called corticosteroids, the major ones being cortisol and aldosterone. Cortisol is made when the body is under stress: during and after illness or injury, during instances of prolonged exposure to cold temperatures, or during sustained, severe emotional difficulties. It causes the body to break down protein and to use it for extra energy—a process the body only undertakes when it expends a lot of energy over a long time or when it lacks other sources of energy—to combat continuing stress. Cortisol is produced when the pituitary gland sends ACTH to the adrenal glands. Aldosterone helps the kidneys, sweat glands, and intestines retain salt in order to balance the body's water and salt levels.

One of the major components of the endocrine system is the *pancreas,* a multipurpose organ that is the body's second-biggest gland (only the liver is larger). As mentioned in Chapter 7, one of its functions is to help the body use sugar by producing the hormone insulin. When the blood has plenty of the sugar glucose in it, insulin helps cells absorb the glucose, stops the liver from sending more glucose to the blood, and helps muscle cells store some excess sugar as glycogen for future energy needs.

If the pancreas does not produce enough insulin, however, these important sugar-using functions are disrupted; the resulting disease is known as diabetes mellitis. In diabetics, or people who suffer from diabetes, a lack of insulin causes too much glucose to remain in the blood instead of being absorbed by the cells. As a result, not only do the cells become starved for energy but the entire chemical balance of the body can become upset, causing damage to a wide range of delicate tissues, including the eyes, skin, nerves, and liver. Some cases of diabetes can be controlled by a special diet in which the sugars are restricted; others require regular (usually daily) doses of artificial insulin, taken either orally or by injection. In most cases, diabetics learn to inject themselves with insulin and learn to carry their syringes and medication with them with minimum disruption of their life. In any case, however, anyone suffering from diabetes should be under a doctor's care because the disease, left untreated, can lead to blindness, coma, or even death.

The *thymus is* a small organ located in the upper chest. Although it is instrumental in the development of antibodies, particularly being the site where T cells (a component of the immune system) develop, the thymus becomes smaller and smaller after puberty. Eventually, it ceases to function at all. Thymus epithelial cells release thymopoietin and thymosin, two hormones that regulate T cell maturation.

The major glands of the reproductive system are the ovaries in the female and the *testes* in the male. The testes' primary function is to produce sperm. The ovaries' main task is to produce ova. When a sperm and ovum combine, the result is the creation of a zygote, which may go on to become a new human being. The reproductive system's glands also make hormones: in females, estrogen and progesterone; in males, testosterone.

Reproductive hormones are responsible for the development of gender characteristics, or those traits that differ in males and females. These include males' deepened voices, facial hair, and external reproductive organs; and, in women, wider pelvic bones, breast development, and smoother skin with less body hair. The reproductive hormones also help control the events of reproduction: release of ova from the ovary in females, development of sperm cells in males, and the events of conception (the merging of sperm and ovum to produce one single new cell), pregnancy, and birth. Because these activities are complex, they will be described in more detail in Chapter 9: The Reproductive System.

Aside from the glands themselves, one other important part of the endocrine system is an area of the brain called the *hypothalamus.* The hypothalamus has a number of complex nervous-system functions, including regulation of sleep and wakefulness, body temperature, and hunger. It also helps regulate the production and release of hormones. Its most direct effect is on antidiuretic hormone, a substance produced in the hypothalamus and sent via special cells into storage centers in the pituitary gland. When cells in the hypothalamus detect excessive amounts of salt in the blood, the hypothalamus signals the pituitary gland to release antidiuretic hormone, causing the body to retain water in order to dilute the salt. When salt levels are too low the hypothalamus does not trigger antidiuretic hormone: the body can then get rid of excess water through urination, and the salt level will rise.

The hypothalamus also monitors blood levels of other hormones and sends chemicals called inhibitory factors (which lower hormone levels) or releasing factors (which raise hormone levels) to hormone-producing glands. The pituitary-produced thyrotropic hormone, for example, is released when the hypothalamus sends thyroid-releasing factor to the pituitary gland. Similarly, other substances are given off by the hypothalamus to stimulate the adrenal glands and the glands of the reproductive system. Thus the hypothalamus acts as a central organizer and supervisor for the glands of the endocrine system.

9

THE REPRODUCTIVE SYSTEM

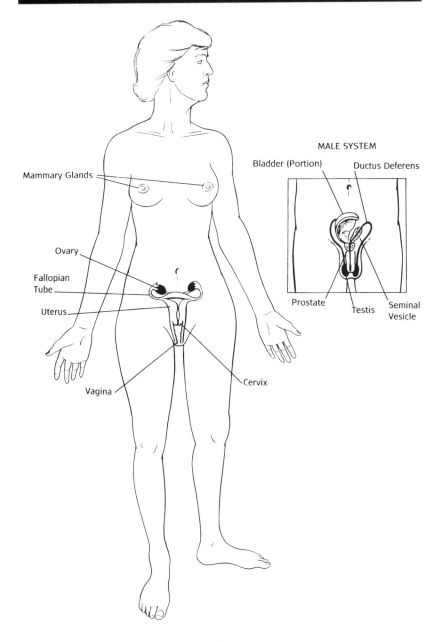

MALE SYSTEM

Bladder (Portion)

Ductus Deferens

Mammary Glands

Ovary

Fallopian Tube

Uterus

Prostate

Testis

Seminal Vesicle

Cervix

Vagina

The reproductive system is the group of specialized organs by which human beings create new life. The development of these organs is different in males than in females because male and female bodies perform different reproductive functions: the male system is designed to fertilize the egg that will grow into a child, whereas the female system is designed to produce an egg each month, support and carry the developing fetus, and nourish the child once it is born. To produce a child, both the female and the male systems work together, making up the whole human reproductive process.

During infancy and childhood, the organs of the reproductive system are present in the body. But these organs do not mature and begin performing reproductive functions—the processes that produce offspring—until about the age of 11 in females, and age 12 or 13 in males. This period is known as puberty and signals the sexual maturation of young adults. Young girls grow body hair in their underarm and pubic areas, their breasts may begin to grow, and they menstruate for the first time. Young boys will also develop hair in their underarm and pubic areas, as well as on their face. Their voice will deepen, their penis (the male sexual organ) will grow larger. It is to be noted, however, that such changes occur in different degrees and at varying times and ages in each individual. All of these dramatic changes, often traumatic in young people's lives, are caused by the release of hormones.

In the male, the organs of the system are the testes, the *prostate,* the *seminal vesicles,* the *epididymis,* the *vas deferens,* and the penis. The function of these components is to make sperm cells (the cells that combine with female cells called ova to make a new human being) and to transport the sperm into the female's body where the combination of sperm and ovum may take place.

The two testes are contained in a loose sac of skin called the *scrotum.* The scrotum holds the testes outside the abdominal cavity because sperm cells, which the testes produce, are sensitive to heat; the warmth inside the body could injure or kill them. Each testis is a tough capsule that contains a network of tiny tubules, the seminiferous tubules. Between the tubules are cells called *Leydig's cells,* which produce hormones called *androgens.* A major androgen is testosterone. Circulating throughout the body in the blood, androgens stimulate and maintain male traits such as deep voice and facial hair, while also spurring the *seminiferous tubules* to produce sperm cells.

The seminiferous tubules produce about 500 million sperm cells every day. Each sperm is so tiny that one drop of fluid can contain about 120 million individual sperm cells. Each sperm consists of two parts: its rounded head contains chromosomes, hereditary instructions that—along with chromosomes from the ovum—will tell the offspring's cells how to develop. The other part of the sperm cell is the tail, a long, hairlike structure; the sperm moves by whipping this tail back and forth. This propelling motion is essential because the penis does not deposit sperm in the female's fallopian tubes (where sperm usually meet ova) but in the vagina, several inches away. So sperm cells must travel in order to reach the ova. A sperm's ability to move—normally, about one inch per minute—is called its motility.

After they are made in the tubules, the sperm cells move to the epididymis, in the outer area of the testis. In this coiled tube the sperm mature for about two weeks. Then they move to the vas deferens, a tube that carries them up into the abdomen. There, the sperm cells are stored behind the lower part of the urinary bladder in a sac called the seminal vesicle. Near the seminal vesicle is the prostate gland. This gland produces fluid that mixes with sperm to make the sperm-carrying fluid called *semen.* Near the vesicle are two glands called *Cowper's glands,* which also contribute fluid to the semen.

From the seminal vesicle, a duct called the ejaculatory duct carries semen to the urethra. This is a tube leading through the center of the penis to the opening at its tip. (The urethra is also the tube that carries urine from the penis. Muscles around the urethra prevent urine and semen from mixing.) The penis also contains blood vessels and groups of cells—tissues—called *erectile tissues.* When erectile tissues fill with blood from the blood vessels, the penis enlarges and stiffens, so that it is easier to insert into the female's vagina during sexual intercourse.

During intercourse, the penis deposits the sperm-containing fluid, semen, into the female's vagina by an act called *ejaculation.* The semen deposited by one ejaculation contains millions of sperm cells. Of these, only about 100 live long enough (a sperm lives about 2 days) to merge with an ovum. The reason for this drastic decrease in sperm is that many sperm cells are killed by the slightly acidic fluids in the vagina; only the strongest survive. Of those that do survive, not all have enough motility to travel very far; less-motile sperm also eventually die. The result is that only the most vigorous sperm—the ones most likely to combine with healthy ova to produce viable offspring—ever reach the female organs to combine with an ovum.

The functions of the female reproductive system are to produce ova; to nourish and protect the unborn child while it grows and develops;

Sperm surround an ovum. Although millions of sperm cells are released during ejaculation, usually only about 100 ever live long enough to reach an ovum, and in most cases only one will succeed in penetrating the ovum's cell wall to fertilize the egg.

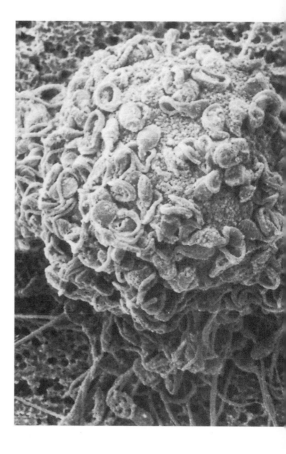

and to send the infant out of the mother's body into the world, in the process of birth.

The main organs of the female reproductive system are the ovaries, the fallopian tubes, and the *uterus.* The ovaries produce the hormones of the female reproductive system, *estrogen* and *progesterone;* circulating in the bloodstream, these hormones control and maintain female body traits, as well as controlling the reproductive organs.

The ovaries also develop and release the ova, sending them into the fallopian tubes, which lead from the ovary to the uterus. The uterus is the muscular, hollow organ where, if an ovum is fertilized, the embryo (as a fertilized egg is called) is nourished and protected while it develops before birth.

Unlike the male reproductive system, which is always producing sperm cells, the female system performs its functions on a schedule, working in a regular cycle of about 28 days. The cycle, called the menstrual cycle, is divided into 2 parts: the *follicular phase* (the first 14 days) and the *luteal phase* (the second 14 days).

A cycle begins when the ovary releases a mature ova. (Unlike the sperm cells of the male, which are constantly being made in the testes, the female body is born with all its ova—about 10,000 of them—already present in the ovaries.) An ova begins maturing in response to the hormone called *follicle-stimulating hormone* (FSH), made by the pituitary gland in the brain. It is released from a structure on the ovary, the follicle, into the fallopian tube.

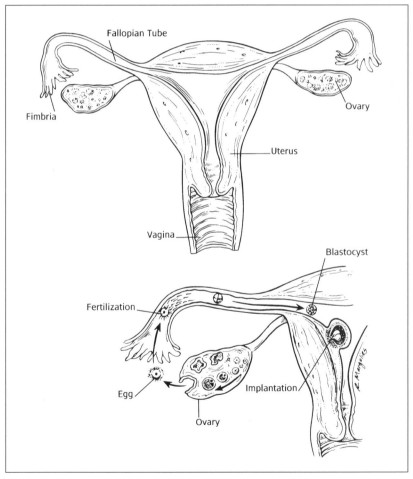

Top: *The female reproductive system.* Below right: *The sperm penetrates the egg in the fallopian tube, and then the fertilized egg travels to the uterus, where implantation takes place.*

Once the ovum leaves the ovary, the follicle itself is stimulated by another pituitary hormone called *luteinizing hormone.* This hormone changes the follicle into a thickened, bright yellow structure called the *corpus luteum;* when it does so, the follicular phase of the menstrual cycle ends, and the luteal phase begins. In the luteal phase, the corpus luteum makes progesterone, which directs the uterus to prepare for receiving the ovum from the fallopian tube.

If sperm cells have made their way from the vagina to the fallopian tube within about two days of the time the ovum left the ovary, the ovum can merge with a sperm cell. This process is called conception, or fertilization. If fertilization occurs, the corpus luteum continues thickening the lining of the uterus, and the sperm/ovum combination, now a single cell called the *zygote,* travels to the uterus, attaches to the uterine wall, and begins growing and developing there.

If fertilization does not occur—if a sperm cell does not meet and merge with an ovum—the thickened lining of the uterus disintegrates and leaves the body through the vagina. The process of discharging the unused material is menstruation. After a menstrual period has ended, the cycle of preparing the uterus for a fertilized egg begins again.

Men continue to produce sperm throughout their life. Women, however, are born with a finite number of eggs. Sometime between the ages of 40 and 60 menstruation will become irregular and then stop altogether. Decreased hormone production may cause the growth of excess facial hair, mood swings, and differences in body temperature (often called hot flashes). This cessation of menstruation, along with its accompanying changes, is known as menopause.

FERTILIZATION

A sperm cell fertilizes an ovum by pushing its round head through the cell wall of the ovum until it is entirely inside. The outer wall of the sperm cell dissolves, and the cells' centers, called *nuclei* (one center is a nucleus) join and mingle their contents. If this happens, where before there were two cells, the sperm and the ovum, now there is only one—the zygote. Its single nucleus contains the chromosomes from both the sperm and the ovum: hereditary instructions that will tell the new cell how to develop into a new human being.

Both sperm cells and ova differ from other cells in that they have only 23 chromosomes in their nuclei, whereas the number of chromosomes in the rest of the body's cells is 46. This enables the sperm/ovum

The human fetus at four months. What began as a single cell is now recognizable as a human. At this stage, however, the fetus cannot survive outside the mother's body.

combination to produce a zygote that has the normal number of chromosomes. So the new cell gets 23 chromosomes from the sperm and 23 from the ovum: half from its father and half from its mother. This is why a person may have, for instance, red hair like his mother and also be tall like his father: All human beings inherit some genetic instructions from one parent and some from the other.

Once sperm and ovum have fused into a single 46-chromosome zygote, the new cell begins multiplying. In the zygote's nucleus, each chromosome divides in half; now there are 92. The chromosomes separate into two sets of 46 each. One set lines up on one side of the nucleus, while the other set lines up on the other side. Now the walls of the zygote's nucleus begin moving together, between the two chromosomes, so the nucleus looks like a figure eight (8). Finally, the 2 halves of the 8 separate to form 2 circles—each a new nucleus containing 46 chromosomes. The cell itself then divides into two cells, and the process continues: the two new cells divide to become four, the four divide to become eight, and so on. In this way, the new individual grows.

Meanwhile, this steadily dividing cluster of cells roots in the tissues of the uterine wall. At the place where it attaches, two structures grow: a tissue called the placenta links the new cell group to the uterine wall, and the umbilical cord, running to the placenta's center, links the blood system of the mother to the developing blood-circulation system of the new human being.

As the cells of the new individual grow, they also differentiate: some cells become different from other cells. The process causing this change is not entirely understood. But by the fifth week of development the specialized tissues of the eyes, face, heart, arms and legs, and some other body parts are formed. At eight weeks the new individual, now called a fetus, is recognizable as a male or female. At week 28 the eyes open, but not until about week 36 is the new human being well able to survive outside its mother's body.

At this age, the fetus is able to breathe air, to digest food, and to circulate oxygen and nutrients with its own blood system. At this point the process of birth begins. The placenta separates from the wall of the uterus, the uterus muscles contract, pushing the infant's body out through the vagina—and a new human being enters the world.

10

THE MUSCULOSKELETAL SYSTEM

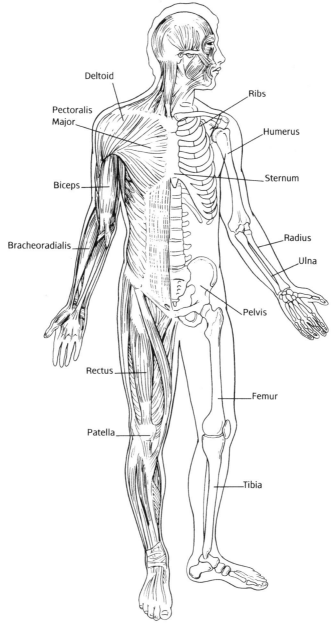

Deltoid

Pectoralis
Major

Biceps

Bracheoradialis

Rectus

Patella

Ribs

Humerus

Sternum

Radius

Ulna

Pelvis

Femur

Tibia

The body's bones make up its skeleton, the solid structure upon which the body as a whole is built. Except for the teeth, the bones are the body's hardest tissues; they give the body its shape and strength as well as protecting many of its internal organs. Some bones also form the blood cells, in soft central bone tissues called marrow.

There are five main kinds of bones in the body: the long bones, such as those in the arms and legs; "short" long bones, such as those in the hands and feet; short bones such as those of the spinal column; flat bones, including skull, rib, *scapula* (shoulder blade), and breastbone; and sesamoid bones, rounded bones such as the *patella* (kneecap).

All bones are made of two main kinds of material tightly meshed together: a framework of cells made by the body itself, called the *osteoid,* or *collagen matrix,* and deposits of minerals—calcium, magnesium, and fluoride—called the *mineral matrix.* Without enough collagen, bones would be too brittle and would fracture easily; without enough minerals, they would be too soft—soft enough to bend. Together, however, the two matrices make bones just stiff enough—not too soft, but not too brittle, either.

A long bone consists of three layers: the central cavity, called the *medulla;* the cortex, made of a hardened outer layer and a spongier inner layer; and the outer coat, called the *periosteum.* The medulla of a long bone is filled with red tissue called marrow, the function of which is to produce the body's blood cells. Marrow is also found in skull bones, ribs, the breastbone, the pelvis (the bony structure between the lower abdomen and the legs), and in the spinal bones.

In the spongy part of a long bone's cortex are canals called *haversian canals,* running down the bones' length and containing their blood vessels and nerves. Around the canals are the *lamellae,* layers of the collagen-and-mineral bone tissue, containing tiny holes called *lacunae.* Within the lacunae are the living bone cells, called *osteoblasts* and *osteoclasts.*

Osteoblasts build bone tissue; osteoclasts dissolve it. Working together, these two types of cells can change bone tissue in response to the body's needs. For instance, if a person takes a job lifting heavy boxes, the arm bones will begin absorbing more stresses from the unaccustomed work. In response, the two types of bone cells "remodel" the bone into a slightly new shape, one with an arrangement of thicker and thinner areas that enable it to do the new work more safely and efficiently. This amazing process occurs in the hard part of the cortex,

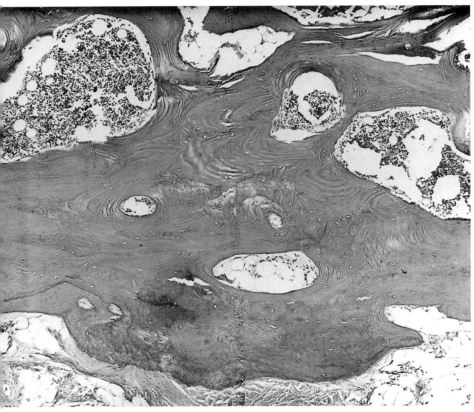

Haversian canals (shown as white circular spaces in the bone tissue) are canals that run down the length of a bone and contain the bone's blood vessels and nerves.

which gives bone its attributes of stiffness and strength. In the regions of the cortex closest to the bone's surface, the osteoblasts deposit more bone tissue; in deeper areas, osteoclasts dissolve and reabsorb bone.

Covering the surface of a long bone is a tough membrane, the periosteum, which supports and protects it at all spots, except at points of contact with other bones. At such contact points, long bones are covered by cartilage: a tough, smooth, flexible substance that allows joints to slide against one another easily. Enclosing the two cartilage-covered bone ends forming some joints is a membrane called the *synovial capsule*. The strong fibrous tissues of the capsule form a sort of sleeve that holds bone ends in proper alignment with one another. Inside the capsule, fluid called *synovial fluid* lubricates the joint.

An X ray of the bones of an adult's hand (bottom) and that of a 6-year-old child's. The area of bone growth—called the epiphysis—is located at the end of each bone and is made up of cartilage membranes that produce cartilage cells that harden into bone as a person matures. This is why a child's hand bones may have space between them, but an adult's appear not to.

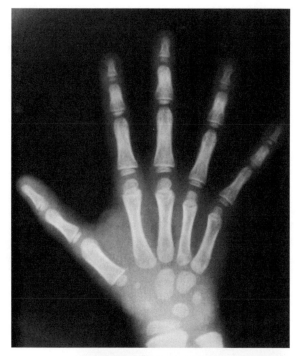

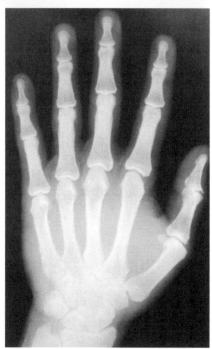

The inner structure of other bones may be somewhat different from that of the long bones, depending upon their location and function. Short bones and flat bones, for example, consist only of spongy cortex surrounded by a thin layer of hard bone, whereas some skull bones contain large air-filled cavities called *sinuses.*

Whatever their structure or function, until the age of about 21 the body's bones must continue to grow. (Even after this point, bones will continue to grow in circumference.) But they must also be hard enough to provide strength and support even at an early age. Bones can perform both functions because of a structure called the *epiphysis.* The epiphyses are cartilage membranes inside growing bones, one near each end. On the inner surface of the epiphysis, cartilage cells are constantly being made and hardened into bone; these push the epiphysis outward, lengthening the bone as a whole as well as lengthening its hardened inner area. This is why the epiphysis is known as the bone's growth plate. When the bone reaches its adult size, newly hardened bone tissue stops pushing the epiphysis outward and instead spreads right through the epiphysis, to the very end of the bone itself. Now, with its whole length hardened, the bone is as long as it will ever get.

The structure formed by all the body's bones is called the skeleton. It is divided into two main parts: the central, or axial, part, consisting of the head and trunk, and the appendages—the arms, hands, legs, and feet. The appendages are connected to the axial skeleton by two roughly circular bone structures: the shoulder girdle, where the shoulders connect to the body, and the pelvic girdle, where the legs connect to bones at the lower end of the trunk.

The two girdles are different in one main way: the arms need free movement but do not have to bear the weight of the body, so the shoulder girdle is not a complete circle of bone (which would give it more strength than it needs) but has many muscular connections (which allow the arms to move in many directions). The pelvic girdle, by contrast, needs strength because it supports the whole weight of the upper body but does not need a wide range of motion (ability to move in many directions). Thus the pelvic girdle is a complete circle of bone, with fewer muscle connections than the shoulder girdle.

Helping to hold the skeletal bones together, providing a framework for bone growth, and adding additional support to the body is cartilage—a flexible, spongy connective tissue. Tendons, also, play a part in

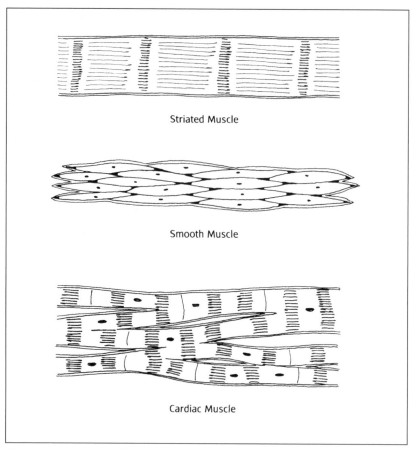

Striated Muscle

Smooth Muscle

Cardiac Muscle

Whereas smooth muscle fibers, involved in involuntary movement, are relatively simple, skeletal (striated) and cardiac muscle fibers are specialized for their more sophisticated functions.

the structure of the body. Tendons are the fibrous cords to which muscles are attached.

The muscles are responsible for the body's ability to move. Other than some primitive movements of blood cells and the whiplash movements of a few hairlike structures (such as the cilia of the respiratory tract), all body movements originate in muscle cells. The importance of the muscles to the body may be judged by the fact that their tissues account for at least half the body's total weight.

Different types of muscles perform the different functions that the body requires. Smooth muscle is responsible for motions that are not under conscious control—body functions that are performed automatically. Digestion is an example of an involuntary muscle function; this process moves food along the digestive tract without a person having to think about it. A single smooth-muscle cell is a narrow fiber about 250 microns long (a micron is one ten-thousandth of a centimeter) with a nucleus in the center; instead of needing stimulation from a nerve, such a cell contracts in response to being stretched.

Striated muscle is the kind of muscle used to move the arms or legs or to perform other voluntary movements. Striated muscles are attached to the bones of the skeleton and are stimulated to move by signals from nerves. Each fiber in a muscle may be several centimeters long (a centimeter is about ⅖ of an inch). Each contains many cells lacking separating membranes and so also contains hundreds of nuclei.

Striated muscles are essential to voluntary movements, which exercises such as gymnastics require.

These muscle fibers are joined by a nerve fiber from the brain or spinal cord. The place where nerve and muscle meet is called the motor end plate, or *myoneural junction.*

Cardiac muscle is the third main kind of body muscle. It makes up the walls of the heart. In a way, like the other muscles, cardiac muscle is connected to the central nervous system as well. In fact, cardiac muscle is part of the autonomic nervous system (an offshoot of the central nervous system), connected through the vagus nerve. Cardiac muscle contracts via stimulation from structures within the heart itself. Cardiac muscles are so tightly meshed together to form the walls of the heart that there is no clear line where one cell ends and another begins.

Whatever their type or function in the body, the job of muscle cells is to convert energy into force. The body's muscle cells take glycogen, the basic unit of chemical storage from carbohydrates, and convert it to energy by breaking the bonds that hold the glycogen molecules together. This bond breaking is done by structures inside the muscle cell called *mitochondria.* The glycogen molecule breaks into smaller molecules of adenosine triphospate (ATP), an energy-storing chemical found in all cells. Mitochondria then break ATP into two even smaller molecules of adenosine diphosphate (ADP). The energy freed by this breakdown is available for the muscles to use in their movement.

Just exactly how muscle cells use the energy is not well understood. But scientists believe it happens somewhat like this: to begin a muscle contraction, nerve signals travel down a nerve to the neuromuscular junction—the place where nerve and muscle cell nearly touch one another. There the impulse liberates the chemical acetylcholine. Flowing across the gap between nerve and muscle cell, acetylcholine causes calcium ions to flow within the muscle cell.

Next, calcium ions spread through the muscle cell to thick and thin muscle filaments arranged opposite one another like the teeth on two combs. The thin filaments are called *actin;* the thick ones are called *myosin.* Upon reaching them, the calcium ions interact with two molecules on the actin filament: *troponin* and *tropomyosin.* First the calcium attaches to the troponin; then the calcium-troponin combination somehow makes the tropomyosin "move over" so that spots on the actin fiber are exposed.

Meanwhile, mitochondria in the myosin fiber break down ATP molecules to ADP molecules, then break down the ADP to release energy. Using this energy, the myosin fibers grab on to the newly exposed actin fibers—and pull. The effect is similar to two combs whose teeth become meshed together, one pulling the other one along. As the pulling continues, the whole muscle cell shortens—that is, it contracts. It is this pulling process that forms the basis for muscle movement.

Once contraction has occurred, the muscle needs a fraction of a second to relax before it can contract again; this time is called a muscle's *refractory period*. If a muscle is stimulated to contract over and over, it uses up all the glycogen it had stored within it for energy and makes more waste product—a substance called *lactic acid*—than it can get rid of. This situation is called muscle fatigue, a situation anyone who has worked until his or her muscles are tired will readily understand. Within a single muscle, some fibers are able to react faster but also get tired faster; these are called fast-twitch fibers. Muscles also contain slow-twitch fibers—slower to respond but also able to contract more times without becoming tired. The lactic acid itself—the stimulated muscle cell's waste product—is responsible for the soreness felt the next day or so after heavy or unusual exercise.

The body's muscular system is made up of hundreds of groups of striated muscles, dozens of smooth muscles, and of course the muscle of the heart—a total of many more than can be detailed in this book. But the striated muscles—the ones controlled by the nervous system and consciously moved—are divided into five main kinds.

Some muscles are *prime movers*—the main bearers of force in a particular kind of movement. The deltoid muscle of the shoulder, for instance, is the prime mover in lifting a barbell overhead.

Agonist and *antagonist muscles* move opposite one another; for instance, when the biceps of the upper arm contracts, the forearm pulls in toward the body; contracting the biceps' antagonist muscle, the triceps, pulls the forearm outward. Muscles that work together like this, called mated muscles, often match an *extensor* (a muscle that pulls a body part away from the main body) with a *flexor* (a muscle that pulls a body part toward the body).

Stabilizing muscles tend to hold bones or other body parts in a steady position, to make a firm base. The abdominal muscles, for instance, hold the hips, back, and lower abdomen up and in line with one another.

Synergistic muscles assist in actions taken by prime mover muscles. A weighlifter's wrist muscles, for instance, hold the wrists stiff; in doing so, they also prevent finger muscles from relaxing. Thus the wrist muscles help the fingers keep their grasp on a heavy weight.

The skeletal system also provides containment—in bone marrow—for one of the body's most amazing processes and the production of cells that defend the entire system from invasion. In the next chapter, the workings of this system—the immune system—will be shown.

11

THE IMMUNE SYSTEM

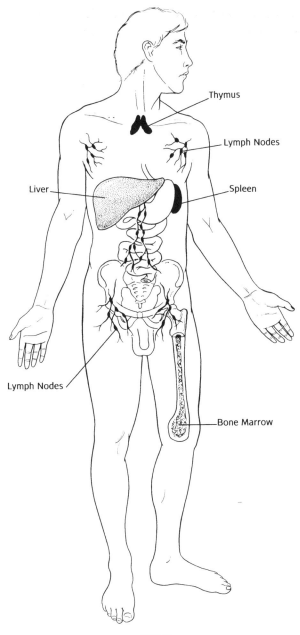

Thymus

Lymph Nodes

Liver

Spleen

Lymph Nodes

Bone Marrow

The immune system is the body's defense system: an array of organs, tissues, cells, and substances that protect it against invasion by foreign material. Viruses, bacteria, pollen, and even some human tissues such as skin grafts or blood transfusions are identified, attacked, and destroyed by the immune system. The system also attacks damaged cells that threaten the body, such as some cancer cells, as well as removing dead or dying cells in which germs can easily grow. In this way, the immune system defends against a wide range of possible threats to health.

The immune system is able to do all this for a number of reasons. First, it can tell the difference between matter that belongs to an individual's body—self—and matter that does not—nonself. This key ability, called *recognition, is* the first part of the immune system's work, being activated when foreign material enters the body. A substance that triggers the immune system, putting it on the defensive, is called an *antigen.*

People's immune systems vary in the number of substances they react to and in the strength of their reactions. Sensitivity to a substance that does not ordinarily pose a danger to the body is called an *allergy.* A person who is allergic to ragweed pollen, for instance, has an immune system that recognizes the pollen as an antigen, even though it is not really harmful. Scientists do not yet fully understand why this malfunction occurs.

The second key immune system ability is called *specificity.* This means the immune system can tell the difference between two very similar kinds of organic material and choose to react against one but not the other. Specificity is made possible by the fact that the molecules of which an invading material is made contain distinct features in certain areas on their surface. The immune system is able to "recognize" these features and thus to distinguish between types of invading substances. This is why vaccinations (shots containing weakened or killed viruses of different ailments, administered to help build immunity to the ailment) against one disease do not make people immune against other very similar diseases. If not for specificity, one vaccine could protect against many more kinds of disease germs. But specificity lets the body raise its defenses against just one specific infection and not waste its energies on similar but less acute problems.

The immune system's third key ability is called *memory.* Because of this ability, once the body has resisted an invasion by a certain kind of

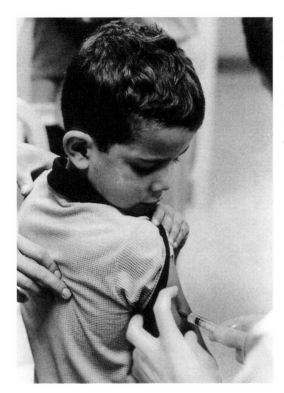

Vaccinations are actually shots that contain weakened or destroyed viruses of different diseases. Once administered, the vaccination triggers the immune system to produce antibodies to that particular disease.

foreign matter, it will recognize and fight that particular type of matter much faster and more effectively the next time. The immune system's memory is the function of special blood cells called memory B cells, which keep circulating in the body after they have reacted against a particular antigen—programmed by the absorption of the antigen itself (by scavenging cells in the blood known as macrophages) to be ready to fight it again. This is why vaccinations protect the body from disease: once a dose of weakened or killed foreign matter triggers and programs the memory cells, they stay alert against that same foreign matter for a very long time, if not for the rest of the person's life.

All three of the key immune system abilities—recognition, specificity, and memory—are the duties of special blood cells called white blood cells, which circulate in the blood and in other channels of the body called *lymph ducts.* Because so many substances and cells work in the immune system, it is easiest to understand the system by seeing it in action—for instance, as it fights off a common cold.

As early as an hour after cold-causing viruses enter nose or throat cells, cells react by making chemicals called *prostaglandins.* Prostaglandins draw white blood cells called *neutrophils* to battle the viruses. When they reach an area of virus activity, neutrophils engulf and digest any viruses they find outside the cells to keep more cells from being invaded.

Neutrophils, which account for two-thirds of the body's whole white blood cell supply, also cause swelling of the infected area. This is an important immune system function because it opens small spaces between invaded cells and capillaries around them. Then plasma (the clear liquid part of blood) can seep into the spaces, carrying more neutrophils to the fight. Plasma raises the temperature in the cells, too— a crucial function, since higher temperatures slow invading germs' reproduction.

The infected cells also release a substance called *histamine*—a chemical that is part of the immune system and also important in the body's pain-sensing nervous system. Histamine makes blood vessel walls more permeable—more like tissue paper and less like waxed paper—so more plasma can seep out of the capillaries. Histamine causes nose cells to secrete more mucus, too, so if more viruses try to invade they will be trapped in the sticky fluid there—another defensive function of the immune system.

If there are not many invaders or if they are not strong, the neutrophils and histamines may kill them all and end the infection. But if many invading organisms survive, two more kinds of white blood cells, the *monocytes* and *lymphocytes,* join the neutrophils in the immune system's fight.

Monocytes are not very numerous, accounting for only about 5% to 10% of all white blood cells, but they make up for their low numbers by being ferocious infection fighters. Stimulated by inflammation at the infected site, they turn into macrophages—a word that means, literally, "big eaters," engulfing and digesting disease germs.

Even more powerful than the macrophages are the lymphocytes, which make up about 25% of the body's white blood cells. When there are no anti-infection battles to fight, the lymphocytes are located in immune system glands called *lymph glands.* When called to battle an infection, they become the powerful weapons of the immune system.

One kind of lymphocyte, the B cell, develops in bone marrow. Making up about 5% of the body's white blood cells, B cells produce

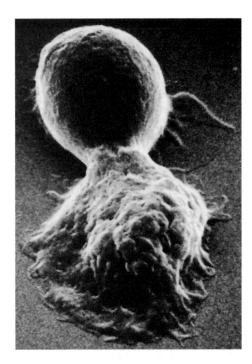

A macrophage engulfs a cancer cell. Macrophages are special white blood cells that travel through the bloodstream and consume antigens—or intruders—before they can further harm the body.

antibodies, or *immunoglobulins,* to prevent viruses from attaching to target cells. B cells also make immunoglobulins that grab on to target cells to stop virus attachment. As mentioned earlier, some memory B cells are responsible for the immune system's memory: they "remember" germs that have attacked before. Memory B cells race to infected cells, get there ahead of invaders, and block them even faster.

The second kind of lymphocyte, the T cell, is also made in the bone marrow but matures in a gland called the *thymus.* (The thymus is located under the breastbone.) Fifteen percent to 20% of white blood cells are T cells. When the inflammation of an infection signals T cells to become active, the T cells change. Some T cells become killer T cells. These attack infected target cells, destroying them before they can release a new crop of invading disease organisms. Others become helper T cells; they cause B cells to make even more immunoglobulins. Finally, some T cells turn into suppressor T cells. They wait until all the invaders have been destroyed, then signal other parts of the immune system to end their fight. This is a vital chore, for without suppressors the immune system would never "turn off," and the body would exhaust itself battling an enemy that no longer existed.

T cells also produce a number of substances that help the immune system fight infections. One is macrophage activation factor, to make macrophages engulf more invaders faster. Another, macrophage migration inhibition factor, keeps the macrophages in the "battle zone." Yet a third is interleukin-2, which causes B cells to produce more immunoglobulins, enhances natural killer cell function, and induces the production of certain types of interferone. Interleukin-2 also seems to attack some cancer cells, and is used as an anticancer drug to destroy tumors, especially in skin and kidney cancers. It is also being tested in combination with other drugs for the treatment of colorectal, ovarian, and certain types of lung cancer.

Another T-cell product, interleukin-1, causes fever. This substance travels in the blood to the brain, which responds by giving the order to "turn up the heat." The body temperature rises, slowing disease-germ reproduction. Higher temperature also increases T-cell and B-cell activity.

Finally, T cells produce interferon—the common name for at least 20 different chemical substances used in the immune system. Against an infection, interferons perform two main chores. First, they spur killer T cells to destroy infected cells. Second, they spur uninfected cells to make antiviral proteins. Although it is not clear why, cells exposed to antiviral proteins do not let viruses take them over. Viruses and other germs may invade a protected cell but still cannot reproduce inside the cell and cannot kill it. Interferons are another group of immune-system substances used in the treatment of a particular type of cancer—hairy-cell leukemia (interferons have also been used in experiments with AIDS, leprosy, the common cold, and a host of other diseases). Interferons are also used in the treatment of chronic hepatitis B and C, and multiple sclerosis.

Besides the main substances and cells of the immune system, there are at least 20 helper proteins circulating in the body's plasma to work against infections. These proteins grab viruses so the macrophages can identify and digest them. They also flag or mark infected, dead, or diseased cells—such as those injured or changed by cancer—for destruction by killer T cells, and they do other chores that help T cells work better. As a group, helping proteins are called the *complement system.*

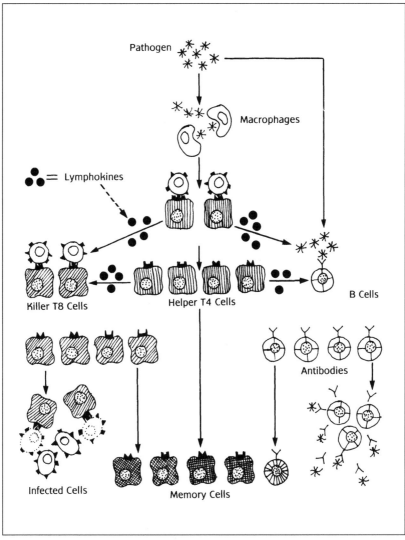

Macrophages engulf immune system intruders, such as pathogens, then relay their antigenic components (internal components are represented as square; external as triangular) to receptors on T cells. Helper T4 cells then multiply and release lymphokines, which regulate both B and T cells. Interaction with T cells and macrophages motivates the killer T8 cells to mature and roam the bloodstream, destroying the infected cells. At the same time, external antigens on the pathogen interact with B-cell receptors. If the B cells receive signals from the lymphokines, they reproduce antibodies that bind to the antigens, neutralizing them. Memory cells (antigen specific) are also created, ensuring that the immune system will more effectively deal with the same pathogen in the future.

The immune system is being investigated with great fervor since the appearance in the late 1970s of the fatal disease AIDS—acquired immune deficiency syndrome—which is caused by a virus that attacks the system's helper T cells. But scientists still have a great deal to learn about the extremely complex and powerful defense system of the human body, so work continues to find out more about the system itself, about the diseases that attack it, and about ways in which it can be used to combat human illnesses in the future.

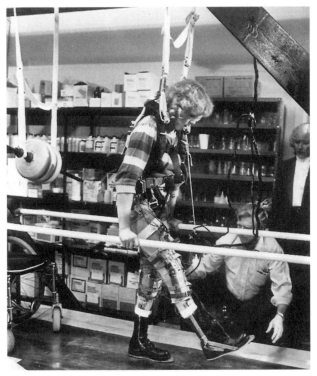

Nan Davis is the first paralyzed person to walk with the aid of a computer.

For all that scientists have discovered about the human body, much more still remains to be learned. They know, for instance, a good deal about the structure of the brain—but just how it functions in thinking, learning, or remembering remains in large part a fascinating mystery. Likewise much is known about how nerves transmit their signals to muscles and how muscle cells get energy from food, but precise details of the mechanics involved in muscle-cell contraction are not yet completely clear.

Perhaps even more astounding is the way the body itself is being improved by advances in modern medicine and technology. Arms and legs lost to injury or disease have in the past been replaced by clumsy artificial limbs—poor substitutes for the real thing. But today, replacements are being developed that can respond to signals from nerves, so the artificial parts of tomorrow will be able to move like real ones. Tiny computerized pumps implanted in the body can give steady doses of insulin to diabetics; thus inconvenient injections of insulin may be replaced by a device that is not only more pleasant to use but which controls diabetes more effectively. Pacemakers—electronic devices long in use to trigger regular heartbeat—can help severely paralyzed people breathe without respirators. In the future, similar but more complex pacers may even help paralyzed people move again, by sending nerve impulses that injured spinal cords can no longer supply.

This technique, called functional electrical stimulation (FES), is under intensive study at an independent study center called the Miami Project to Cure Paralysis. Founded in 1985 by a few Miami doctors, the project has grown to include some 60 physicians and 200 spinal-cord-injured people from around the country. In functional electrical stimulation, a computer sends tiny electrical signals to muscles to make them contract in the same order as they would have if they were getting the signals from the spinal cord. Paralyzed patients whose muscles are connected by wires to the stimulators can pedal stationary bikes, for example, to exercise muscles that would otherwise shrivel from disuse.

Such stimulators have been attached to walkers—metal frames a paralyzed person can lean on in order to stand up. By pressing buttons on the walker, a paralyzed patient can electrically stimulate first one leg, then the other, and actually walk. Such stimulators are still being perfected and it takes a long time and a great deal of hard work on the patient's part to learn to use a walker. And although researchers are unsure of whether or not such walkers or other methods offer hope to older paralyzed patients, they feel sure that young people currently paralyzed will one day walk again.

"Suppose a cure does take another five or ten or even twenty years," physiologist Mark Nash of the Miami project pointed out in *Discovery* magazine. "That means our fifteen- and twenty-year-olds [patients] could begin getting out of their wheelchairs when they're still in their thirties."

Finally, the artificial heart—although not successful in permanently replacing the real organ—is being used as a bridge to keep severely heart-damaged patients alive until they can receive a new heart via yet

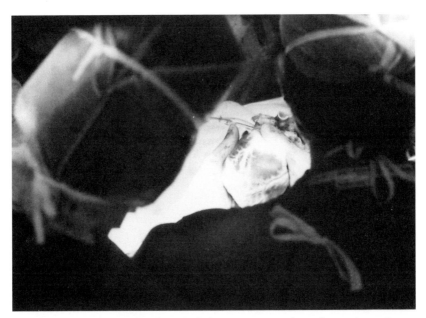

Surgeons at Columbia Presbyterian Hospital prepare to transplant a human heart. Organ transplantation is one of the most dramatic medical developments of the 20th century.

another "improved body" development: the organ transplant. Organ transplants—perhaps the 20th century's most dramatic achievement— are becoming almost commonplace. Today, people can receive new kidneys, livers, hearts, digestive organs, pancreases, bones, retinas, and lungs or heart-lung and other organ combinations. Progress is also being made in skin and nerve transplants. The progress of such transplants, like other medical advances of this era, is a product of steady, determined, and rapidly advancing knowledge about all the body's systems and especially the immune system—whose function must be even better understood for transplant science to continue its rapid advance.

Although modern knowledge of the body and skill in repairing its malfunctions have surpassed the dreams of our ancestors, it is still best to have a healthy body that does not need new parts or other repairs— and the best ways to achieve that are still the old-fashioned ways: sufficient rest, regular exercise, a balanced diet, regular medical checkups, avoiding smoking and other damaging habits such as drug use and excessive drinking, and overall hygiene. For as has been shown, the human body is a complex and marvelous thing—one which, when cared for properly, can ensure many years of healthy, active life.

In the future, many more mysteries are sure to be solved about the human body—its systems and their functioning, its ailments and new ways of curing them. Until then, young people and their families can feel confident in knowing that our knowledge of the human body is more detailed, comprehensive, and useful today than it has been at any time in human history.

APPENDIX

FOR MORE INFORMATION

The following is a list of organizations and associations that can provide further information on the human body and on the functions of its systems.

The Human Body in General
American Cancer Society
1599 Clifton Road NE
Atlanta, GA 30329
(800) ACS-2345
www.cancer.org

American Medical Association
515 N. State Street
Chicago, IL 60610
(312) 464-5000
www.ama-assn.org

Canadian Cancer Society
10 Alcorn Avenue, Ste. 200
Toronto, ON M4V 3B1
Canada
(416) 961-7223
www.cancer.ca

Public Citizen Health Research Group
1600 20th Street NW
Washington, DC 20009
(202) 588-1000
www.citizen.org
(Publicizes important health findings through the media; makes available to the public a broad spectrum of research and consumer action materials in the form of books and reports.)

Society for Adolescent Medicine
1916 NW Copper Oaks Circle
Blue Springs, MO 64015
www.adolescenthealth.org

Society for Developmental Biology (SDB)
9650 Rockville Pike
Bethesda, MD 20814
(301) 571-0647
http://sdb.bio.purdue.edu

United Network for Organ Sharing (UNOS)
P.O. Box 13770
Richmond, VA 23225
(800) 24-DONOR
www.unos.org

U.S. Centers for Disease Control
Public Inquiries Branch
1600 Clifton Road
Atlanta, GA 30333
(800) 311-3435
www.cdc.gov

National Institutes of Health
Public Inquiries
9000 Rockville Pike
Bethesda, MD 20892
(301) 496-4000
www.nih.gov

The Circulatory System
American Heart Association (AMA)
7272 Greenville Avenue
Dallas, TX 75231
(800) AHA-USA1
www.americanheart.org

The Digestive System

American Digestive Health Foundation
7920 Woodmont Avenue, 7th Floor
Bethesda, MD 20814
(301) 654-2635
www.gastro.org

American Liver Foundation
75 Maiden Lane, Suite 603
New York, NY 10038
(800) 465-4837
www.liverfoundation.org

National Digestive Diseases Information
    Clearinghouse (NDDIC)
2 Information Way
Bethesda, MD 20892
(301) 654-3810
www.niddk.nih.gov

The Endocrine System

Endocrine Society (ES)
4350 East West Highway, Suite 500
Bethesda, MD 20814
(301) 941-0200
www.endo-society.org

International Society of Endocrinology
51–53 Bartholomew Close
London EC1A 7BE
England
0171 606 4012
www.jingo.com/ise/ice2000.htm

The Immune System

American Association of Immunologists
9650 Rockville Pike
Bethesda, MD 20014
(301) 530-7178

American Red Cross AIDS
Educational Office
1730 D Street NW
Washington, DC 20006
(202) 737-8300
www.redcross.org

National Jewish Center for Immunology
    and Respiratory Medicine
1400 Jackson Street

Denver, CO 80206
(303) 338-4461
(800) 222-LUNG
www.njc.org

The Musculoskeletal System

American Orthopaedic Association
    (AOA)
6300 North River Road, Suite 505
Rosemont, IL 60018
(847) 318-7330
www.aoassn.org

American Society for Bone and Mineral
    Research
1200 19th Street NW, Suite 300
Washington, DC 20036
(202) 857-1161
www.ashbmr.org

National Multiple Sclerosis Society
733 Third Avenue
New York, NY 10017
(800) FIGHT-MS
www.nmss.org

The Nervous System

Brain Research Foundation (BRF)
134 South LaSalle Street
Chicago, IL 60603
(312) 759-5150

National Institute for Neurological and
    Communicative Disorders and Stroke
National Institutes of Health
9000 Rockville Pike
Bethesda, MD 20205
(301) 496-4000
www.nih.org

Society for Neuroscience
11 Dupont Circle NW, Suite 500
Washington, DC 20036
(202) 462-6688
www.sfn.org

The Reproductive System

Planned Parenthood Federation of
    America, Inc.
810 Seventh Avenue
New York, NY 10019

(212) 541-7800
www.plannedparenthood.org

Society for the Study of Reproduction
(SSR)
1526 Jefferson Street
Madison, WI 53711
(608) 256-2777
www.ssr.org

The Respiratory System

American Lung Association (ALA)
1740 Broadway
New York, NY 10019
(212) 315-8700
(800) LUNG-USA
www.lungusa.org

Canadian Lung Association
75 Albert Street, Suite 908
Ottawa, Ontario K1P 5E7, Canada

(613) 237-1208

1900 City Park Drive, Suite 508
Blair Business Park
Gloucester, ON K1J 1A3
Canada
(613) 747-6776
www.lung.ca

The Urinary System

American Urological Association
1120 North Charles Street
Baltimore, MD 21201
(401) 727-1100
www.auanet.org

National Kidney Foundation (NKF)
30 East 33rd Street, Suite 1100
New York, NY 10016
(800) 622-9010
www.kidney.org

The National Institutes of Health is made up of a number of individual branches that may also provide information. Among them are:

National Cancer Institute
National Eye Institute
National Heart, Lung and Blood
  Institute
National Institute of Allergy and
  Infectious Diseases
National Institute of Arthritis and
  Musculoskeletal and Skin Diseases
National Institute of Child Health and
  Human Development
National Institute of Dental Research
National Institute of Diabetes and

Digestive and Kidney Diseases
National Institute of Environmental
  Health Sciences
National Institute of General Medical
  Sciences
National Institute of Neurological
  and Communicative Disorders
  and Stroke
National Institute on Aging
National Library of Medicine
Office of AIDS Research
Office of Disease Prevention

General Health Hot Lines and Help Lines

American Cancer Society
(800) ACS-2345
American Council for the Blind
(800) 424-8666
(202) 467-5081 (in District of Columbia)
American Heart Association
(800) 242-8715

American Kidney Fund
(800) 638-8299
American Liver Foundation
(800) 465-4837
The Better Hearing Institute
(800) EAR-WELL

National AIDS Hot Line
(800) 342-AIDS
National Health Information
  Clearinghouse
(800) 336-4797

National Jewish Hospital/National
  Asthma Center
(800) 222-LUNG

APPENDIX

FURTHER READING

Asimov, Issac. *The Human Body: Its Structure and Operation.* New York: New American Library, 1963.

Bolt, Robert J. *The Digestive System.* New York: Wiley, 1983.

Campbell, Ann, ed. *The Opposite Sex: The Complete Guide to the Differences Between the Sexes.* Topsfield, MA: Salem House, 1989.

Cherniak, Reuben M., M.D., Louis Cherniak, M.D., and Arnold Naimark, M.D. *Respiration in Health and Disease.* 3rd ed. Philadelphia: Saunders, 1983.

Chitty, Mary Glen, comp. *Federal Information Sources in Health and Medicine: A Selected Annotated Bibliography.* Westport, CT: Greenwood, 1988.

Davis, Goode P. *The Heart: The Living Pump.* Washington, DC: U.S. News Books, 1981.

Dwyer, John M. *The Body at War: The Miracle of the Immune System.* New York: New American Library, 1989.

Elgin, Kathleen. *The Heart.* New York: Franklin Watts, 1968.

The Encyclopaedia Britannica. 15th ed. New York: Encyclopaedia Britannica, Inc., 1998.

Farndon, John. *The All Color Book of the Body.* New York: Arco, 1985.

Horton, Edward, and Felicity Smart, eds. *The Illustrated Encyclopedia of Family Health.* New York: Marshall Cavendish, 1983.

Illustrated Stedman's Medical Dictionary. 24th ed. Baltimore: Williams & Wilkins, 1982.

Jaroff, Leon. "Stop That Germ." *Time,* May 23, 1988, 56.

Kitzinger, Sheila. *The Complete Book of Pregnancy and Childbirth.* New York: Knopf, 1996.

Kluger, Jeffery. "The Miami Project." *Discover,* September 1988, 70.

Kraus, David. *Concepts in Modern Biology.* Rev. ed. New York: Globe, 1998.

LeVay, David. *Human Anatomy and Physiology.* Kent, England: Hodder & Stoughton, 1981.

Lucente, Frank E., and Gady Har-El, eds. *Essentials of Otolaryngology*. 4th ed. Phila.: Lippincott, Williams & Wilkins, 1999.

Lutjen-Drecoll, Elke, and Johannes W. Rohen. *Atlas of Anatomy: The Functional Systems of the Human Body*. Phila.: Lippincott, Williams & Wilkins, 1998.

Marieb, E.N. *Human Anatomy and Physiology*. 3rd ed. Redwood City, CA: Benjamin Cummings, 1995.

Memmler, R. et al. *The Human Body in Health and Disease,* 7th ed. Phila.: Lippincott, 1992.

Mylander, Maureen. *The Great American Stomach Book*. New York: Ticknor and Fields, 1982.

National Institutes of Health. *Understanding the Immune System*. Bethesda, MD: National Institutes of Health, 1988.

Noonan, David. *Life on the Frontlines of Brain Surgery and Neurological Medicine*. New York: Simon & Schuster, 1989.

Rothfeder, Jeffery. *Heart Rhythms*. Boston: Little, Brown, 1989.

Silverstein, Alvin. *Itch, Sniffle & Sneeze*. New York: Four Winds Press, 1978.

———. *The Respiratory System*. New York: Twenty First Century Books, 1995.

Singer, Charles, and E. Ashworth Underwood. *A Short History of Medicine*. New York: Oxford University Press, 1982.

Smith, Anthony. *The Human Body*. New York: Discovery, 1999.

Smith, James John, and John P. Kampine. *Circulatory Physiology: The Essentials*. 3rd. ed. Phila.: Lippincott, Williams & Wilkins, 1990.

Stone, Robert J., and Judith A. Stone. *Atlas of Skeletal Muscles*. 3rd ed. New York: McGraw-Hill College Div., 1999.

Tanagho, Emil A. *Smith's General Urology*. 15th ed. New York: McGraw-Hill, 1999.

GLOSSARY

Acetylcholine: A neurotransmitter that helps nerve impulses travel between nerve cells and across the gap between nerve cells and muscle cells.

Acoustic: Having to do with sound and the sense of hearing.

Adrenaline: A hormone that causes blood vessel constriction, increased heart rate, and other reactions that help the body meet emergency situations.

Afferent message: Nervous system signal from the body to the brain.

AIDS: Acquired immune deficiency syndrome; an acquired defect in the immune system thought to be caused by a virus (HIV) and spread by blood or sexual contact; leaves people vulnerable to certain, often fatal, infections and cancers.

Allergy: An inappropriate and harmful response of the immune system to normally harmless substances.

Anatomy: The study of the way the body is structured.

Antigen: A bacteria, virus, or other foreign substance that causes the body to form an antibody.

Aorta: The largest artery in the body.

Arteriole: Any of the small terminal vessels of the artery that end in capillaries.

Artery: A blood vessel that carries blood away from the heart.

ATP: Adenosine triphosphate; an energy-storing compound involved in metabolism; found in muscles as storage space for extra muscular energy.

Atrium: Either section of the upper area of the heart, which is divided into left and right chambers.

Axon: The message-sending part of a nerve cell.

Bacteria: Microscopic unicellular organisms.

B cells: B lymphocytes; immune system cells that produce IgE.

Blood pressure: The force with which blood pushes against blood vessels and other body structures.

Bone marrow: Red tissue, inside some bones, the function of which is to make blood cells.

Bronchus: Either of the two large air tubes in the trachea.

Capillaries: Microscopic blood vessels that link arterioles with venules.

Cell: A mass of protoplasm, containing a nucleus, that alone or while interacting with other cells is capable of performing all the life functions.

Central nervous system: The part of the nervous system that includes the brain and the spinal cord.

Cerebrospinal fluid: The clear fluid that surrounds the brain and spinal cord; acts mainly as a shock absorber.

Chromosomes: Rodlike structures found in the nucleus of mammalian cells that contain the genes; each human cell (except gametes) contains 23 pairs of chromosomes.

Cranial nerves: Twelve pairs of nerves directly connected to the brain.

Dendrite: The message-receiving part of a nerve cell.

Diastole: The period between heartbeats, when the heart muscle relaxes.

Digestion: The process of breaking food into simpler chemical components for use by the body's cells.

Dissection: The process of cutting apart an object or organism for study.

DNA: Deoxyribonucleic acid; genetic material, located in all cells as double strands of paired nitrogenous bases, that contains the codes for an organism's inherited characteristics; most genes and chromosomes are made of DNA.

Efferent message: A nervous system signal from the brain to the body.

Electron: An elementary unit of electricity; negatively charged particle of the atom.

Embalming: Preservation of a corpse against decomposition.

Endocrine system: The glands located throughout the body that produce hormones and secrete them directly into the bloodstream.

Exocrine: Relating to the secretion or production of substances that are given off via ducts and tubes to specific areas of the body outside of the producing glands.

Fetus: The developing human from nine weeks after conception to birth.

Fistula: Abnormal passage leading from the surface of the body to an internal cavity or from one organ to another.

Ganglia: Knobby groups of nerve cells on the outside of the spinal cord that send messages up the spinal cord to the brain.

Gastric juice: A thin, watery, acidic, digestive fluid secreted by the glands in the mucous membrane of the stomach.

Glia: The nonnervous or supporting tissue of the brain and spinal cord.

Glycogen: A complex carbohydrate molecule used primarily for energy storage; fuels muscles.

Hemoglobin: A substance in red blood cells that binds with oxygen and carbon dioxide in order to transport them through the bloodstream.

Hormone: A substance carried in the bloodstream that regulates many bodily processes, modifying both structure and function of other substances or cells that play roles in these processes.

Immune system: The body's mechanism for combating viruses, bacteria, and other outside threats; composed of various types of white blood cells, including phagocytes, which consume bacteria, and lymphocytes, some of which produce antibodies.

Immunoglobulin: One of several globular proteins produced by the immune system to act as antibodies.

Interferon: One of several proteins that enhance immune system activity; production can be stimulated by such things as viral infection or the presence of certain bacteria or protozoa.

Ion: A molecule that carries a small electrical charge.

Lacteal: Relating to milk.

Limbic system: Group of structures of the brain that are concerned with emotion and motivation.

Macrophage: A type of white blood cell that destroys invading cells or foreign particles by engulfing them.

Membrane: Thin layer of tissue covering or dividing an organ or cell.

Metabolism: The process by which the body, or a cell, gains energy from food and uses it for the functions of life.

Mucus A thick white substance secreted by mucous glands.

Myelin: A fatlike substance forming a sheath around the axons of certain nerves.

Myoneural junction: The place where a nerve cell transmits its signal to a muscle cell.

Nervous system: The body system that is made up of the brain and the spinal cord, nerves, ganglia, and parts of the receptor organs and that receives and interprets stimuli and transmits impulses to the effector organs.

Neuron: A nerve cell.

Neurotransmitter: A chemical that carries nerve signals across the gaps between nerve cells or between nerve cells and muscle cells.

Nociceptor: Nerve endings that sense pain.

Nucleus: Area in the center of a cell, usually enclosed in a membrane, that is an essential agent in growth, metabolism, reproduction, and transmission of genetic characteristics.

Olfactory: Having to do with the sense of smell.

Optic: Having to do with sight.

Osmosis: The process by which a substance moves through a membrane from an area of high concentration to an area of low concentration.

Ovum: Egg cell; female gamete.

Parasympathetic nervous system: Part of the autonomic nervous system that induces secretion of substances and contraction of smooth muscles and causes dilation of blood vessels.

Periosteum: The outer covering of a bone.

Peripherial nervous system: The outer branches of the nervous system, i.e., the nervous system except for the brain and spinal cord.

Peristalsis: The muscular contraction that moves food through the digestive tract.

Physiology: The study of how the body works.

Placenta: The organ that develops during pregnancy to supply the fetus with oxygen, food, water, and nutrients from the mother's bloodstream and to carry waste back to the mother's body for disposal.

Platelets: Blood cells that control clotting.

Pulmonary circulation: The route of blood from the heart, to the lungs where it is oxygenated, and then back to the heart.

Respiration: Movement of oxygen from atmosphere to cells and carbon dioxide from cells to atmosphere.

Rods and cones: The light-sensing cells in the eyes.

Saliva: Fluid secreted by the salivary glands of the mouth that begin the process of digesting food.

Sclera: The white of the eye.

Skeleton: The structure formed by the body's bones.

Smooth muscle: Muscle tissue that lacks striations; involuntary muscle tissue.

Sperm: Male gamete.

Spinal chord: Part of the nervous system that transmits impulses to and from the brain.

Striated muscle: Muscle fibers that contain alternating light and dark bands; mainly voluntary muscle tissue.

Sympathetic nervous system: The part of the autonomic nervous system that is concerned with preparing the body to react to situations of stress or emergency.

Synapse: The gap between nerve cells.

Systemic circulation: The route by which blood flows from the heart, to the organs and tissues that receive much of the blood's oxygen in exchange for carbon dioxide, and then back to the heart.

Systole: The time during which the heart is pumping a beat, when the heart muscle contracts.

T cell: T lymphocytes; cells that signal other lymphocytes to attack invading cells or chemical structures foreign to the body.

Thymus: Glandular structure in the chest where T cells mature.

Trephination: The process of cutting a hole in the skull to relieve pressure on the brain.

Vaccine: A substance made of killed or weakened bacteria or virus that will stimulate the body to create antibodies against the disease caused by the same bacteria or virus; these antibodies increase an individual's immunity to a particular disease.

Valve: Structure which prevents backward flow in a passage.

Vein: A blood vessel that carries blood from the body back to the heart.

Vena cave: Either of two large veins—superior or inferior—by which blood is returned to the right atrium of the heart.

Ventricle: Either of the two lower pumping chambers of the heart.

Venule: Any of the minute veins connecting the capillaries with the larger veins.

Virus: A minute acellular parasite composed of genetic material (either DNA or RNA) and a protein coat; viruses cause such diseases as polio, measles, rabies, and smallpox.

Zygote: Fertilized egg cell.

INDEX

APPENDIX

PICTURE CREDITS

cover: Fred Burrell/Science Source/ Photo Researchers
13: Debra P. Hershkowitz
15: Spencer Grant/Taurus Photos
17: National Library of Medicine
19: The Bettmann Archive
20: The Bettmann Archive
22: The Bettmann Archive
25: Original illustration by Robert Margulies
27: Martin M. Rotker/ Taurus Photos
28: Original illustration by Gary Tong
30: Martin M. Rotker/ Taurus Photos
33: Original illustration by Robert Margulies
35: Courtesy of The Fragrance Foundation
36: SIU/Peter Arnold Inc.
37: Original illustration by Marjorie Zaum
39: Phiz Mezey/Taurus Photos
40: Courtesy of Northern Metropolitan MRI
43: Original illustration by Gary Tong
45: Karen R. Preuss/Taurus Photos
47: Original illustration by Robert Margulies
48: Laimute Druskis/ Taurus Photos
51: Martin M. Rotker/ Taurus Photos
52: Original illustration by Robert Margulies
55: Original illustration by Robert Margulies
57: Original illustration by Robert Margulies
60: Richard Wood/Taurus Photos
62: Original illustration by Robert Margulies
63: David M. Phillips/Taurus Photos
65: Original illustration by Robert Margulies

67: Frank Siteman/Taurus Photos
69: Martin M. Rotker/ Taurus Photos
70: Courtesy of National Heart, Lung, and Blood Institute/National Institutes of Health
73: Original illustration by Robert Margulies
75: Courtesy of The Upjohn Co.
77: Debra P. Hershkowitz
78: Martin M. Rotker/ Taurus Photos
81: Original illustration by Robert Margulies
84: E. S. Beckwith/Taurus Photos
85: Martin M. Rotker/ Taurus Photos
86: Spencer Grant/Taurus Photos
89: Original illustration by Robert Margulies
92: David Scharf/Peter Arnold Inc.
93: Original illustration by Robert Margulies
95: Petit Format/Nestlé/Science Source/ Photo Researchers
97: Original illustration by Robert Margulies
99: Martin M. Rotker/ Taurus Photos
100: Martin M. Rotker/ Taurus Photos
102: Original illustration by Gary Tong
103: Richard Wood/Taurus Photos
107: Original illustration by Robert Margulies
109: Phiz Mezey/Taurus Photos
111: Courtesy of The Upjohn Co.
113: Original illustration by Nisa Rauschenberg
115: UPI/Bettmann Newsphotos
117: UPI/Bettmann Newsphotos

Mary Kittredge, a former associate editor of the medical journal *Respiratory Care,* is a freelance writer of nonfiction and fiction. She is certified as a respiratory-care technician by the American Association for Respiratory Therapy. She has been a member of the respiratory-care staff at Yale-New Haven Hospital and Medical Center since 1972. Ms. Kittredge was educated at Trinity College, Hartford, and the University of California Medical Center, San Francisco. She is the author of *The Respiratory System* in the Chelsea House 21ST CENTURY HEALTH AND WELLNESS series, and of young-adult biographies *Marc Antony, Frederick the Great,* and *Jane Addams.* Her writing awards include the Ruell Crompton Tuttle Essay Prize and the Mystery Writers of America Robert L. Fish Award for best first short-mystery fiction.

Sandra L. Thurman, a graduate of Mercer University, is the Director of the Office of National AIDS Policy at the White House. For more than a decade, Ms. Thurman has been a leader and advocate for people with AIDS at the local, state, and federal levels. From 1988 to 1993, Ms. Thurman served as the Executive Director of AID Atlanta, a community-based nonprofit organization that provides health and support services to people living with HIV/AIDS. From 1993 to 1996, Ms. Thurman was the Director of Advocacy Programs at the Task Force for Child Survival and Development at the Carter Center in Atlanta, Georgia. Most recently, she served as the Director of Citizen Exchanges at the United States Information Agency. She is a recognized expert on AIDS issues and has provided testimony before the United States Senate, the White House Conference on HIV/AIDS, and the National Commission on AIDS.

C. Everett Koop, M.D., Sc.D., currently serves as chairman of the board of his own website, www.drkoop.com, and is the Elizabeth DeCamp McInerny professor at Dartmouth College, from which he graduated in 1937. Dr. Koop received his doctor of medicine degree from Cornell Medical College in 1941 and his doctor of science degree from the University of Pennsylvania in 1947. A pediatric surgeon of international reputation, he was previously surgeon in chief of Children's Hospital of Philadelphia and professor of pediatric surgery and pediatrics at the University of Pennsylvania. A former U.S. Surgeon General, Dr. Koop was also the director of the Office of International Health. He has served as surgery editor of the *Journal of Clinical Pediatrics* and editor in chief of the *Journal of Pediatric Surgery.* In his more than 60 years of experience in health care, government, and industry, Dr. Koop has received numerous awards and honors, including 35 honorary degrees.